excuse me

excuse me

THE SURVIVAL GUIDE TO
MODERN BUSINESS ETIQUETTE

Rosanne J. Thomas

AMACOM

AMERICAN MANAGEMENT ASSOCIATION

New York • Atlanta • Brussels • Chicago • Mexico City • San Francisco
Shanghai • Tokyo • Toronto • Washington, DC

American Management Association: www.amanet.org
This publication is designed to provide accurate and authoritative information in regard to the subject matter covered. It is sold with the understanding that the publisher is not engaged in rendering legal, accounting, or other professional service. If legal advice or other expert assistance is required, the services of a competent professional person should be sought.

Library of Congress Cataloging-in-Publication Data
Names: Thomas, Rosanne J., author.
Title: Excuse me : the survival guide to modern business etiquette / Rosanne
    J. Thomas.
Description: New York : AMACOM, [2017] | Includes index.
Identifiers: LCCN 2016059931| ISBN 9780814437919 (hardcover) | ISBN
    9780814437926 (ebook)
Subjects: LCSH: Business ethics.
Classification: LCC HF5387 .T476 2017 | DDC 395.5/2--dc23 LC record available
    at https://lccn.loc.gov/2016059931

About AMA
American Management Association (www.amanet.org) is a world leader in talent development, advancing the skills of individuals to drive business success. Our mission is to support the goals of individuals and organizations through a complete range of products and services, including classroom and virtual seminars, webcasts, webinars, podcasts, conferences, corporate and government solutions, business books, and research. AMA's approach to improving performance combines experiential learning—learning through doing—with opportunities for ongoing professional growth at every step of one's career journey.

10 9 8 7 6 5 4 3 2 1

FOR JEAN

contents

CONTENTS

introduction

Growing up, I cannot recall ever hearing my parents mention *etiquette*. A fussy word that conjures up a certain level of affectation, it was likely not the first one that came to mind for my parents who were otherwise involved in the care, feeding, and general management of six children. Yet respectful behavior—the actual manifestation of good etiquette—was indeed mentioned and modeled by my parents continually, and expected of us every day. Of course, being considerate of our siblings was not our first inclination. As kids vying for attention or the last piece of pie, sharing and waiting our turns were not second nature to us. But we did our best because we knew such behaviors were nonnegotiable.

In our family, manners lessons came in many forms. Our naval officer dad would often remind us to "take all you want, but eat all you take" (military-ese for not being greedy or wasteful) and not to "short-stop" (when passing food, not to help yourself first, especially if it is the last serving). Our high-school teacher mom let us know that the correct response when she called our names was "Yes?" not *"What??"* She reminded us that "please" and "thank you" were not to be omitted and that arguing was a nonstarter.

One of my fondest childhood memories was of our mom and dad bravely piling us into our big station wagon on Friday nights and taking us to a local Italian restaurant for dinner. A huge treat for us, we were fully cognizant that any future excursions depended entirely upon how well we behaved. Since no one child *dared* jeopardize this for the rest, we rose to the occasion every time. And we learned how to twirl spaghetti in the process! We also learned—to our amazement—that this whole concept of showing good manners had an upside. Good things *and* ice cream came to those who were polite.

This trip down memory lane may evoke similar reminiscences from those who also came of age sometime in the 20th century. We remember when parents were shown respect simply because they were *parents*. We recall how family dinner was sacred: Everyone showed up on time, hands cleaned, and ready to participate in a family discussion. At these meals, children learned how to hold their forks and knives, how to speak when it was their turn, and how to listen when it was someone else's turn. Telephone calls were never taken. When outside the home, people dressed up for school, church, and travel; showed respect for authority; and with most audiences, generally kept their language profanity-free.

Much of what constituted respectful behavior a generation or two ago seems positively quaint by today's standards, with little relevance in the 21st century. Back then, parents were parents, and friends were friends, and never the twain did meet. Today, many parents *are* their children's best friends, and vice versa. Then, showing respect for authority figures such as adults, teachers, and employers was simply done. Today, the very idea of authority is questioned. Then, sit-down meals were a nightly ritual. Today, coordinating schedules and dietary preferences to make such an event happen seems like far too much work.

In other ways, though, civility in the 21st century looks very much like it did before, even if its tenets are now applied in different ways. Today, we hear about the importance of *authenticity* and *transparency*. Back then, it was known as telling the truth. Today, *teamwork* is the mantra. Back then, you couldn't win a game of touch football without it. Today, organizations are embracing *conversation cultures*, as though conversing with colleagues is a new workplace invention. Last century, there were expectations of appropriate attire and behavior on the job. Today, there still are, even if they are defined in new ways.

Of course, much has changed—dramatically. In the 20th century, questions about how to refer to a gay colleague's spouse, whether it was okay to text the boss at home over the weekend, or how to handle a checkered online past did not come up because the situations did not yet exist.

Add to this the generational challenge, as millennials—considered digital natives because they grew up with digital technology—try to work side by side with digital immigrants: traditionalists, baby boomers, and Gen Xers. These generations speak different languages, hold different values, and have different goals. Some say that because of the sheer number of millennials and their presumed influence, a new playbook for workplace behavior should be designed predominantly with this group in mind. But millennials are still outnumbered by the previous generations combined, and the previous generations are still mostly in charge. Gen Z is also coming up fast. Soon, there will be *five* generations needing to figure out how to work together.

In a workplace rife with opportunity for misunderstanding, people often do the wrong thing, at great expense to relationships and reputations. Workplace incivility—unintentional or sometimes deliberate—is rampant. Nine out of 10 employees say they have experienced or witnessed incivility on the job. And it's costly. "Job stress, much of which stems from workplace incivility, costs U.S. corporations $300 billion a year."[1]

How do employee populations come together with such disparate ways of looking at the work environment today? How are best behavioral practices identified to mitigate misunderstandings and ensure everyone feels understood and heard within a corporate culture? How do individuals and organizations burnish personal and company brands to position themselves most competitively in a fiercely competitive global arena? It's a tall order, but it *can* be done. It requires adoption of a new playbook for workplace behavior that respects the individual, which in turn paves the way for the greatest mutual success.

Excuse Me takes on this challenge. Incorporating dozens of real-life scenarios, hundreds of practical tips, valuable advice from those on the front line, and resources for additional information, *Excuse Me* explores what it takes to survive—and thrive—in today's demanding global workplace. It takes a look at the root of workplace disrespect, from corporate cultures and the behaviors they allow to the uncertainty in interacting with coworkers of different genders, races, sexual orientations, cultures, physical abilities, and backgrounds.

A respectful workplace is a more pleasant workplace, and there are very real bottom-line advantages that accrue to organizations that uphold them. Eric Imparato, a principal at the accounting firm Wolf & Co., said, "In a commodity market-place, it's easy to translate skills into shareholder value. People are differentiated by how they behave and can charge greater rates as a result."

As readers go through these pages and consider the in-numerable ways they are evaluated in the workplace, they may find themselves thinking, "Uh-oh, I should have been doing that" or "Whoa, I definitely should *not* have been doing that!" Have readers made missteps? If they are anything like me, they have—and will again. This is understandable. There is a great deal of new information to absorb and realities to accept. These, combined with everyday work and life stresses, create an ideal environment for interpersonal missteps.

The very good news is that the practice of on-the-job etiquette does not require anyone to be perfect. It only requires a good faith effort to know and do the right thing, and when one errs, to employ the all-powerful apology to right the ship. We will need others to excuse us as we get up to speed with new business expectations and the needs of the various workplace populations, just as we will excuse those who are trying their level best to do the same. We will not dwell on past transgressions—ours' or others'—but instead simply identify opportunity areas for growth and change and make continuous improvements toward our objectives.

My goal for readers is that they develop confidence in them-selves and in their interactions with others and feel empowered to bring their best, most authentic selves to the workplace each and every day. *Excuse Me* makes it everyone's responsibility to treat everyone else with respect and civility. Because when employees feel respected and valued, individuals and organiza-tions win.

excuse me

respect

Practicing the Platinum Rule

"I've learned that people will forget what you've said, people will forget what you did, but people will never forget how you made them feel."

—MAYA ANGELOU

She hasn't been even one week on the job at Push Hard Marketing and 23-year-old Abby knows she made a huge mistake. There had been warning signs. Her new employer's rating on Glassdoor was a mere 2.9 out of 5. The interviewer's vagueness about the team, the manager, and even why this sought-after position was available all raised red flags. But the website's job description dovetailed perfectly with her interests and education, and the company billed itself as collaborative and inclusive, all major advantages in Abby's book. And besides, she needed a job.

Her reception is chilly. One week in, virtually no one has spoken with her. Her questions illicit one-word answers or shrugged shoulders. There is a supposed "welcome to the team" meeting about to begin, but the manager is late. The team members wait. Some glance furtively in Abby's direction. One has his eyes glued to his iPhone. Another grouses that he's got better things to do. Then Abby overhears a complaint about having to break in *another* new hire.

The manager finally arrives and launches immediately into the team's dismal quarterly results, telling them they have three months to turn things around or they'll all be looking for new jobs. And, "Oh, by the way, make sure you get your new team member up to speed." The manager gets a call and leaves. The team unleashes a diatribe about their clueless boss before the meeting deteriorates into a cacophony of complaints and interruptions.

While they completely ignore Abby, she decides, then and there, that she will start her new job search *today.*

We are all familiar with the ancient and venerable Golden Rule, which impels us to treat others as we would wish to be treated. While noble, in today's world and workplace of diverse ages, cultures, sexual orientations, experiences, preferences, goals, and lifestyles, the Golden Rule falls short. Its basic premise is that there is only one frame of reference—one's own—for determining how another would like to be treated. A newer rule, the Platinum Rule, goes one big step farther by requiring truly respectful people to treat others as *they* would wish to be treated. Dr. Milton J. Bennett, founding director and CEO of the nonprofit Intercultural Development Research Institute, introduced the term in his 1979 article, *Overcoming the Golden Rule: Sympathy and Empathy.* Dr. Bennett says the Golden Rule is based on an assumption of similarity between individuals while the Platinum Rule assumes there are differences.[1]

By most accounts, the workplace has a way to go toward the widespread adoption of the Platinum Rule—or the Golden Rule, for that matter. Whether accidental or deliberate, the lack of respect in the workplace is a pervasive, serious, and costly problem. Inroads are being made as organizations expand inclusion strategies, but there is still a great deal of work to do.

Real Respect

Jane, an administrator at well-respected Bay Farm Hospital, had been looking forward to this year's healthcare conference. Many of her colleagues will be there, and she'll have a chance to network with peers from the world's leading hospitals. The luncheon is an open-seating buffet, and Jane sees Phil, who she knows casually from her hospital, at a table with a free spot. She asks if she can join him and the four other men at the table. Phil nods, quickly introduces Jane, and then continues to regale the group with the very "blue" sexist joke he is telling.

As Phil reaches the end of his joke, he inserts Jane's name in the punch line. Phil, laughing loud and proud of how clever he is, at first does not realize no one is laughing with him. When he finally notices the embarrassed looks on the other men's faces and the horror on Jane's face, he tries in vain to salvage the situation. With a forced laugh, he announces to the table, "Way to ruin a punchline, Jane!"

The foundation of civility is respect, which is the outward expression of esteem or deference. This is the foundational requirement and, without that, no other behaviors ring true. Respect extends to peoples' privacy, physical space, property, viewpoints, philosophies, religion, gender, ethnicity, physical abilities, background, age, beliefs, and personality. Respect and disrespect can be shown by language, gestures, and actions.

Respect is what employees say they want most from their employers and coworkers: respect for their experience, education, intelligence, skill, creativity, hard work, dedication, and the results they produce. Yet respect is what employees say they get least.

Employees, management, and organizations at large are characterized by the behaviors they exhibit and allow. Disrespectful behavior runs the gamut from neglecting basic civilities and outright rudeness to discrimination and bullying. Throughout managements' ranks, disrespect manifests itself with favoritism, subtle pressure, condoning damaging behavior or speech, neglecting to follow up on complaints of harassment or bullying, and criticizing or firing employees who voice concerns. Organizations that engage in illegal or unethical activities, such as deceptive business practices, embezzlement, and predatory pricing, and the cultures such activities create, also contribute to this problem.

It's not enough to say an organization values respect and civility. The boss who preaches the importance of respectful listening without practicing it is better off saying nothing at all. Dr. Todd Whitaker and Dr. Steve Gruenert, professors of educational leadership at Indiana State University and authors of the book *School Culture Rewired,* say, "The culture of any organization is shaped by the worst behavior the leader is willing to tolerate."[2] It stands to reason that a culture would also be shaped by the best behavior a leader is willing to model.

An incredible 80 percent of employees believe they get no respect at work, and a whopping 95 percent report they have experienced or witnessed disrespect in the workplace,[3] according to Christine Pearson and Christine Porath, authors of the book *The Cost of Bad Behavior.* Mike Miles, head of social strategy for online retailer SmartSign, said in his article "Workplace Bullying Costs Companies Billions, Wrecks Victims' Health" that the price tag to the U.S. economy for all of this bad behavior is an estimated "360 billion annually due to turnover and decreased work productivity."[4]

Disrespect also comes in subtle forms through *microaggression*. Dr. Derald Wing Sue, Ph.D., professor of counseling psychology at Columbia University, defines microaggressions as "the everyday verbal, nonverbal, and environmental slights, snubs, or insults, whether intentional or unintentional, which communicate hostile, derogatory, or negative messages to target persons based solely upon their marginalized group membership."[5] Reflecting unconscious bias, a microaggression can be a "compliment" to an African American colleague on how articulate he is or a remark to a female executive on how impressively she balances work and family responsibilities.

Workplace disrespect affects employees' morale, engagement, productivity, and health. It also negatively affects coworkers who witness it, causing them stress and job insecurity. It becomes contagious, creating a greater likelihood of rudeness throughout the employee population. Disrespected employees are more likely to leave jobs, increasing their companies' severance and benefits pay, recruiting, hiring, and training costs, and potentially, legal fees. As Dr. Robert J. Cuomo, Ph.D., dean and professor of business at Dean College, said, "People don't leave jobs. People leave people." Disrespect ruins companies' reputations, loses customers, and eats up managers' valuable time.

The benefits to companies that establish genuinely respectful cultures are enormous, including everything from greater productivity and increased bottom lines to happy shareholders.

The enhanced reputation of a respectful organization means it is able to hire and retain the best and brightest, resulting in a distinct competitive advantage. Teamwork, trust, and creative problem solving are also fostered, and employees realize greater job satisfaction, self-respect, and even enhanced earning potential.

Employers must enforce a zero-tolerance policy in order to realize the benefits of a respectful culture. The law now protects victims of the most egregious forms of disrespectful behavior, but how much better it would be not to need to rely upon the law for enforcement. Management can educate employees on the company's Code of Respect and invest in civility training to make sure all employees understand the policy.

Employers need to look closely at their hiring practices. Carefully watching for behavioral clues during the interview process and not hiring candidates with red flags is easier, faster, and less costly than dealing with them after they are hired. The candidate who casts blame on a former employer, exhibits disrespectful body language, or comes across as arrogant during the interview can be expected to display the same or worse behavior once hired. Employers can hire for "attitude over experience" as the Four Seasons does, or heed the call of Howard Schultz, CEO of Starbucks, for civility and values-based leadership. They can emulate the practices of *Fortune's* "100 Best Companies to Work For" and view corporate culture as their greatest tool.

Employees, on the other hand, need to know bosses mean what they say. Management should encourage the reporting of disrespectful behavior without fear of consequences. This can be achieved through anonymous 360-degree reviews or by identifying an HR representative or independent workplace consultant to whom employees can make confidential reports.

And if disrespect is reported, management must confront it specifically and immediately and take appropriate action.

Companies can reward good behavior with positive reinforcement. At Zappos, employees who show exemplary behavior can earn "Zollars" (Zappos dollars) and peer-to-peer "Wow" awards from their coworkers. Anything from holding a door open, to smiling, volunteering, or cleaning a common area might qualify someone for a $50 reward. Regularly scheduled employee recognition luncheons, holiday parties, and summer outings that bring together various employee populations can do wonders to build trust. Bosses can also publicly recognize and value employees for their ideas and accomplishments and reward initiative and creativity.

Most important, bosses must consistently model the behavior they want to see in their employees. Smart bosses recognize that treating employees with respect is critical to attracting and retaining workers. They also realize that what happens at work does not stay at work. Sites like glassdoor.com, which has a database of more than 8 million company reviews, enable job seekers to evaluate rankings of companies' cultures and values *before* deciding whether or not to join their ranks. At such sites, salary and benefits reports, CEO rankings, interview questions, and insights into what it's really like to work at a company are all at a job seeker's fingertips.

Employees also need to do their part, beginning with becoming aware of any unconscious biases they may harbor. Recently, I had a personal experience with the concept of unconscious bias. While walking home through the Boston Common from the gym early one morning, I heard a voice say, "Hey, lady, you don't have to be afraid." Lost in thought, it took me a second to realize the person was talking to me. I stopped and walked toward two African American men sitting on a bench. I said I was not afraid and asked them why I would be. One man said, "When you saw us, you walked to the other side of the sidewalk." I assured him I did not; he assured me I did. What ensued was a remarkable 15-minute conversation about the concept of unconscious bias. We exchanged names and parted as new friends, promising to pick up our conversation if our paths crossed again. In continuing to think about what happened, I know for sure I was unaware of any bias. But did I cross to the other side of the walkway? I simply do not know. This question, and its lesson, have stayed with me.

Employees can embrace everyone's uniqueness and extend simple common courtesies such as listening attentively and valuing others' opinions. While not always easy, they can also challenge disrespect when they experience or witness it. When you witness what you think is disrespectful or exclusionary behavior, it is important to assess the situation to make sure you are reading it correctly. Once you are certain, it's time to take action. Depending on the seriousness of the situation, you could try to diffuse it with humor by saying something like, "Don't hold back. Tell us how you really feel!" Such an approach might get an interaction back on a respectful track. If this does not work, you'll need to be more direct. You could say, "Something seems to be bothering you. What is it?"

To improve a relationship, you could say, "I want us to work well together. How can we do that?" If someone interrupts you, you could say, "Hold on . . . I'd like to make my point." If someone displays aggressive body language, you could say, "You look upset. What's wrong?" If someone uses inappropriate language, you could say, "Can we rein in this discussion? We're at work." If someone is spreading gossip, you could say, "I was surprised to hear you said (something) about me. Is that true?" And if someone is blatantly rude, you could say, "You may not realize how negative that sounds." Sometimes none of these work, in which case it's time to get management or HR involved.

Once the personal and institutional groundwork for showing respect has been laid, we are ready to consider what respect means to the various populations of today's workplace.

Respect for Experience

Bill takes a deep breath and braces himself for today's weekly staff meeting. Sixty-five years old, Bill is a workplace survivor. He has lasted 42 years with the same large bank and has had nine different bosses and seven different jobs in four different locations. He has assiduously played the political game, always keeping his head down. Bill has risen through the ranks to management and enjoys a comfortable salary.

Bill knows the workplace has changed dramatically and has tried, as much as possible, to keep up. Despite his best efforts, he still cannot seem to connect with his much younger staff. At last week's meeting, Bill rolled out a new marketing plan that Josh, the new hire, immediately questioned before offering a "much better idea." Drew asked for feedback on a project but seemed put off by Bill's constructive suggestions. Colin, three months on the job, asked Bill, again, when he would be promoted. Gina said she hadn't prepared a report for the meeting because she doesn't listen to voicemail or read email, and in the future, would Bill please text her.

Bill has tried very hard to stay current. He's taken Salesforce and database management training and mastered Excel. He's up to speed on social media and active on LinkedIn. He knows he has a lot of experience to share, but somehow his staff treats him like a "has been," as though he should just retire. But with a couple of kids still in college, that is not an option for Bill. So he squares his shoulders and enters the meeting room. He will continue to try and relate to his staff as well as he can—he has to.

Millennials are the fastest growing, most sought-after demographic in the workplace. By 2020, there will be 86 million millennials in the workplace, representing 40 percent of the total working population.[6] Should a new business etiquette playbook be designed exclusively with them in mind?

The simple answer is no. Millennials, born roughly between 1981 and 2000, are still outnumbered by traditionalists, baby boomers, and Generation Xers combined. And these folks are still largely in charge. According to statisticbrain.com, the median age of an S&P 500 CEO is 55.[7] Warren Buffet and J. Willard Marriott, Jr., are in their 80s and 90s, with countless lesser known CEOs in their 70s and 60s. The U.S. retirement age is also going up. A 2014 Gallup survey reports that the average age at which non-retired Americans expect to retire is 66,[8] the highest age Gallup has found since first asking the question in 1991. What's needed is a new playbook for respect that acknowledges the perspectives and values of all ages, not the least of whom are those still making the hiring decisions and signing the paychecks.

The current four generations in the workplace come from distinctly different social, political, and business times in history. Their perspectives evolved as they were exposed to people, places, and ideas, but were still largely informed by the prevailing social mores of their formative years. The great disruptor, digital technology, has only widened the gap. While opinions differ on their precise characteristics and birth years, the following represents generally held views of the generations.

Traditionalists

Born before 1946, traditionalists joined a work world where women were primarily in support roles and social behavior was the template for business behavior. Men traditionally showed respect to women by doffing their hats, holding doors open, pulling out chairs, paying bills, and refraining from vulgar speech. The flip side of the coin was a kind of *Mad Men* approach to women, job and wage discrimination, and bias along lines of race, religion, class, age, marital status, and sexual orientation. Traditionalists are respectful of seniority and rank and are loyal, disciplined, and self-sacrificing. Technology for this cohort consisted of a radio, a rotary telephone, and a television.

Baby Boomers

Born between 1946 and 1964, baby boomers came of age between the mid 60s and the early 80s. They witnessed or participated in the civil rights movement. The Equal Opportunity Act of 1972 was enacted when the first of the boomers were in their 20s. By 1986, when the last of the boomers had entered the workplace, more than half of college graduates were women taking their places beside men in traditionally male-dominated fields such as law, medicine, and business. Acceptable behavior on the job was changing dramatically. It was no longer considered appropriate to focus on gender rather than ability. Boomers, while less respectful of rank, still believe in corporate hierarchy and strive to climb the corporate ladder. Touch-tone telephones were one of the technological innovations of their time.

Generation X

Born between 1965 and 1980, Generation X entered the workplace in the mid 80s. The Civil Rights Act (1991) and the Americans with Disabilities Act (1990) were both enacted while they were in their 20s. Astronauts Sally Ride, a woman, and Guion Bluford, an African American man, broke ground by going to space during this time. Members of Gen X were the first to have two parents work outside of the home in great numbers. They also saw many of those parents lose their jobs. As a result, this generation does not have the same respect for job titles or rank, nor do they believe in job security. Known for being distrustful, self-reliant, and tech-savvy, Gen Xers are protective of family time and value work-life balance. They were the first to experience mobile technology.

Generation Y/Millennials

Born between 1981 and 2000, Gen Y/millennials do not remember a time before mobile devices. Entrepreneurial and tech-savvy, they have fostered relationships with people all over the world through social media. Laws enacted as this generation grew up and came of age included the Family and Medical Leave Act in 1993, same-sex marriage in Massachusetts in 2004, and the Lilly Ledbetter Fair Pay Act in 2009. Millennials value diversity and social responsibility and are known for being especially close to their parents. They'd like to make more money, but seem less concerned about that than about making a difference.

Respecting Age Difference

The need and desire for respect, appreciation, and acceptance cut across generational divides. By taking the time to learn about other generations, we can begin to embrace rather than judge or discount others' experiences and points of view and realize the vast personal and professional benefits that accrue to us in doing so. Younger generations can also keep in mind that if they're lucky, one day they will *be* part of the older generation and that karma—good or bad—may await them!

Respect for Diversity

Ginny didn't sleep well last night. New to her job as an event planner, she is due to meet with her boss today and needs to steel herself to discuss the evaluations from last week's annual clients' conference in New York.

Ginny knew from the initial tepid response that attendance would be low. But she had not anticipated so many complaints from those who did attend about everything—the food, the venue, the transportation, the speakers—virtually the entire conference had been panned. She realizes in hindsight that if she had put a little more thought and research into the conference, she would have saved herself a lot of trouble.

She had been pleased to find a great rate, within her budget, at a fabulous hotel for the last week in March, but she completely failed to anticipate that Passover and Easter, coinciding this year, would affect turnout. She thought she'd covered her bases with food by offering two menu selections: a vegetarian and beef option. It had not occurred to her to request that vegan and kosher meals also be available. She had made sure that the entrance to the venue was accessible but did not think to see if there were some low cocktail tables or if the coach she'd hired was accessible for people with disabilities. She thought the speakers she had invited represented an interesting mix of experience, but it had not occurred to her that they were all middle-aged white men.

Ginny prepared for the likelihood that the meeting with her boss would be as much of a disaster as the conference had been. Now she was wondering if this first meeting would be her last.

Today's workplace has many faces, and those faces have changed considerably since the oldest of the workforce first entered. Approximately 70 years ago, non-Hispanic white men made up about 80 percent of the workforce. Today, the workplace is approximately 66 percent non-Hispanic white, 16.4 percent Hispanic, 11.7 percent African American, and 5.8 percent Asian.[9] Census data tells us that by 2050, there will be no racial or ethnic majority in the U.S.[10] In general, most respectful behaviors are appropriate for all employees, but some groups require different or additional considerations.

Diversity refers to race and ethnicity, but also to gender, sexual orientation, persons with disabilities, and former military. Women make up 46.8 percent[11] of the workforce today. In 1950, it was just 29.6 percent. Gay and transgender workers represent another 6.28 percent of the workforce, persons with disabilities, 5.5 percent, and former military, 9 percent.[12] Employers have embraced diversity, not only because it is the law, but also because a diverse workplace is a productive, adaptive, competitive, and innovative one. But there are challenges.

Gender Respect

Make no mistake; sexism is still alive and well. An older male employee of an insurance claims office tells a young female colleague that he'd love to have a "front-end collision" with her. A recent college graduate who works for a high-end clothing retailer is given some "friendly advice" by her boss: If she wants to get promoted, she will have to lay off the cookies. Management doesn't promote "fat girls." A top producer at a tech company rebuffs advances from her male boss and is then passed over for promotion, because she is not a "team player." A young male employee has an impressive physique. His female boss responds by squeezing his bicep. The older male coworker is expected, yet again, to pick up the check at lunch.

Men and women in the workplace represent close to a 50-50 split, and mutual respect is imperative. Yet sexual harassment and sexist behavior, illegal and unacceptable as they are, still exist. While men are considered the main culprits, women may also be guilty of sexist behavior toward men or even toward other women. Language, presumptions, or behavior that relegates particular responsibilities or excludes, demeans, or offends based on gender is considered sexist, no matter who the perpetrator is.

It is critical that employees present a united front against sexist behavior in the following ways: Eliminate the use of sexist labels such as men are "assertive" and women are "aggressive." Reject sexist expectations such as women make coffee, arrange celebrations, and take office collections, while men change water coolers, lead meetings, and open doors. Don't exclude based upon gender by inviting only women to join book clubs, take cooking classes, or get pedicures, or by inviting only men to join golf outings, have after-hour drinks, or play cards. Don't use sexist language, tell sexist jokes, or make sexist presumptions. And finally, scrupulously avoid offering unwelcome compliments, unwanted advances, and making any inappropriate gestures, gazes, stances, or touching. In a nutshell, treat all coworkers respectfully, professionally, and the same, regardless of gender.

Cultural Diversity

You notice, at a departmental meeting, that your Japanese colleague does not look you in the eye. At a business lunch, your German client frowns when you address him by his first name. At the company Christmas party, your Indian guest seems not to appreciate the leather picture frame you give him. The new proposal you send to your Argentinian business partner garners no immediate response, and when you meet, it seems to take him forever to get down to business. And now your Middle Eastern prospect fails to show up at an important meeting. What is happening here?

As businesses become part of the global arena at an increasing rate, it is vital that we understand how cultures differ and how respect is shown for those whose backgrounds are unlike our own. Everything, including history, language, religion, value systems, communication style, formality of interactions, business practices, greetings, humor, and attitudes toward hospitality, time, money, minorities, women, and age could be startlingly different. Successful professionals accept and embrace these differences, rather than challenge them, paving the way for mutually respectful and successful relationships.

In showing respect across cultures, we want to remember we are dealing with individuals first and cultures second. It is a mistake to assume that "Asians think this" and "Latin Americans do that." It is important to learn as much as possible about other cultures, but this information is to be used to help us understand individuals, not to define them.

Begin by researching colleagues' or business partners' cultures of origin, and by asking questions and showing genuine interest in the answers provided. In conversation, listen patiently and speak slowly, at a normal decibel level. Avoid using nonverbal communication such as the "thumbs up" sign, which is considered offensive in the Middle East, or the "A-okay" sign, which is an obscene gesture in Brazil.

In verbal communication, avoid sarcasm, humor, and words that could be easily misunderstood. Stay away from potentially controversial topics, such as politics, religion, and human rights. Above all, avoid showing judgment or disapproval or comparing cultures in any negative ways.

The LGBT Community

In 2014, Apple CEO Tim Cook came out as gay, "forever changing the game for equality in corporate culture," according to Sara Kate Ellis, president and CEO of GLADD.[13] Indeed, the Lesbian, Gay, Bisexual, and Transgender (LGBT) community is coming out in the workplace as never before and in the process, contributing to the continued shattering of the "glass closet."

Building relationships with and avoiding inadvertent offense to the LGBT community requires that employees educate themselves. Steve Petrow, *Washington Post* columnist and author of *The Essential Book of Gay Manners and Etiquette*, says the questions he receives for his column "Civilities" "reflect both the confusion of the social landscape and the hurt and anger caused by bullying and discrimination."[14] But he says respect and kindness go a very long way.

To show respect for your LGBT colleagues and business partners, educate yourself by learning the correct terminology. Refer to members of the LGBT community in the ways *they* wish to be referred and if unsure, ask. There are now 56 ways in which Facebook users can identify, including "gender questioning," "intersex," "androgynous," and "neither." Facebook spokesman Will Hodges said, "While to many, this change may not mean much, for those it affects, it means a great deal."[15]

Refer to married colleagues appropriately. In the past, married same-sex couples were often referred to as partners or spouses. With the 2014 changes in the Defense of Marriage Act, *husband* and *wife* are now the legal and appropriate terms, and are used unless a couple indicates that they prefer otherwise. And if a colleague has a boyfriend, girlfriend, or fiancé(e), use that term, not *friend* or *roommate*.

If an LGBT colleague is celebrating an engagement, marriage, promotion, or new baby, home, or job, offer congratulations and join in the celebration. Do not ask an LGBT colleague personal questions, offer religious advice, suggest counseling, tell offensive jokes, use inappropriate language, or—need it be said—whisper, gossip, stare, make fun of, or exclude.

It is critically important to keep an LGBT coworker's confidence, especially if he or she has not come out to all. Finally, be an ally. In her article "How to React When Someone Comes Out: Dos and Don'ts for Straight Allies," Miranda Perry of Care

2, a social network website for activists, says, "If you're straight, you can be an ally by creating a safe space for them to come out. You'll help combat homophobia and transphobia, and support the LGBT people in your life—even those you may not know about yet."[16]

People with Disabilities

Well-intentioned individuals sometimes make mistakes that range from the comical to the offensive when interacting with colleagues with disabilities. According to United Cerebral Palsy, "the rules of etiquette and good manners for dealing with people with disabilities are generally the same as the rules for good etiquette in society."[17] It cautions that everyone is different, however, and that its published guidelines hold true for *most individuals most of the time.*

United Cerebral Palsy recommends that one speak directly to a person with a disability, not a caregiver, and shake hands if possible (using left hands is fine). If someone is unable to shake hands, another physical greeting such as a tap on the arm or shoulder is appropriate. Adults are always to be treated as adults. The National Center on Workforce Disability advises using "person first language" such as *person with a disability* instead of *disabled* or *handicapped.* It advises respecting all assistive devices and animals, such as canes, wheelchairs, crutches, and service dogs, and using a normal speaking tone and style.

When speaking with someone who is visually impaired, identify yourself and others with you. When speaking with a person who is deaf, look directly at the person, and then speak clearly, slowly, and expressively. When speaking with someone using a wheelchair, place yourself at eye level. There is a wealth of additional information available that will ensure interactions with people with specific disabilities are helpful, positive, and professional.

Most importantly, display the right attitude. Never pity or assume someone is unhappy with his life, or exhibit fear or apprehension. Do not presume someone's disability has affected his intelligence, comprehension, memory, job effectiveness, sense of humor, or interests. And finally, relax! Do not be embarrassed to use common expressions that seem to relate to someone's disability such as "See you later" or "I've got to run." People with disabilities use similar phrases all of the time.

According to the Center for American Progress, approximately 38 million Americans have severe disabilities. Workers with disabilities are nearly twice as likely to be unemployed as their nondisabled counterparts.[18] Employers can take advantage of the underutilized talents and vast potential contributions of this population by creating an accepting, understanding, and inclusive culture.

Veterans

Adjusting to a new life is challenging under any circumstances and is especially so for a veteran who may be dealing with physical, emotional, financial, and family issues in addition to the pressures of a new job. There are a number of things coworkers can do to make this transition easier. They can welcome a new colleague by inviting him to coffee, lunch, or after-hours events. They can ask how his transition is going and express interest in his military work experience. They can (and must) avoid asking prying questions ("Do you have service-related physical or emotional issues?") or judgmental questions ("How could you have left your family for so long?").

The Brain Drain

Traditionalists and baby boomers are retiring, cutting back, or moving on to new careers. And unless organizations figure out a way to harvest and transfer their institutional knowledge and relationships, they are going with them. "Brain drain" is an enormous risk to the bottom line and another important reason employers need to ensure respectful communication among generations while there is still time.

The first year all baby boomers were at least 50 years old was 2014. Eighty million strong, they possess the greatest amount of institutional knowledge and represent the largest pool of mentors in the workplace today. Granted, many boomers do not expect to retire until their late 60s, and some have no plans to ever retire. But employers cannot rely on boomers staying on as a way to protect their intellectual capital. Many are leaving for better opportunities, beginning new careers, and starting new businesses. And they are taking their lifelong professional experiences with them.

Employers and coworkers who want to capture this knowledge need to act fast. John A. Challenger, CEO of Challenger, Gray & Christmas, Inc., the outplacement and career transitioning firm, said, "With the leading edge of the Baby Boomer generation reaching age 68 in 2014, it is critical that companies understand their exposure to brain drain related to retirement."[19] There are now roughly two times as many boomers in the workplace as there are Gen Xers. When the retirement floodgates open, there is a legitimate concern that there will not be enough qualified mid-level workers ready to take their places. Those who are ready will be in great demand, and able to command larger salaries as a result.

Employers should communicate with their over-50 employees to evaluate their skills, knowledge, contacts, and retirement plans in order to gauge and limit their company's exposure to brain drain. They can offer creative solutions to those who do not necessarily want to retire but would like less demanding jobs or schedules. Sabbaticals, flexible time, shared responsibilities, and fewer hours—the work-life integration benefits so important to millennials—may be enough to entice these individuals to stay on. They can create a mentoring program to ensure the succession of vital institutional knowledge and relationships to the next generations. They can also "hire for age" by replacing retiring baby boomers with employees of similar backgrounds and levels of experience.

Savvy younger employees can also avail themselves of the treasure troves of information sitting next to them by asking questions and truly listening to answers. Not only are experienced coworkers a font of company information, they have career-spanning relationships with people to whom they might just be willing to make introductions. While gathering information, younger workers want to remember to show patience and express gratitude for the time, advice, and perspective their senior colleagues are willing to offer them. They can also offer advice in a reciprocal mentoring mode.

REMEMBER

- **A culture of respect comes first.** Liberal and consistent application of the Platinum Rule makes this possible.
- **Life experiences inform attitudes and behaviors.** We must challenge our own mindsets and make room for others' backgrounds and beliefs.
- **Diversity is to be embraced.** Its value to individuals and organizations is incalculable.

chapter 2

social skills

Putting Your Best Foot Forward

"I will prepare and someday my chance will come."

—ABRAHAM LINCOLN

Mary, head of Human Resources, has been interviewing candidates all month for a good position at Stellar Insurance Company but still hasn't found the right person. Her boss has run out of patience. "We need an underwriting assistant now!" he tells her. "Choose the best candidate and get 'em in here first thing Monday morning."

Mary reviews the candidates. There was the college grad who asked Mary what the company did exactly. There was the woman who said if she could not bring her cat to work, there was no point in continuing the conversation. Then there was the young man who brought his mother into the interview room for "another set of ears." Mary also recalled the middle-aged man who arrived, unapologetically, 20 minutes late. He told Mary he was completely overqualified but needed a job, so he'd take it. And then there was Chloe.

Chloe had the right skill set, but her appearance was alarming. A snake tattoo coiled up her arm to her neck, in homage, she said, to her pet snake Rumplesnakeskin. She had multiple piercings in her ears and wore a tank top sans bra and flip flops with glittery blue nail polish on her toes. But Chloe was the best of the lot. So Mary offered her the job on one condition: that she come to work appropriately dressed for a conservative insurance company.

First thing Monday morning, Mary gets a call from her boss. "May I see you in my office—now?" he asks, with unmistakable anger in his voice. Mary rushes to his office and sees Chloe sitting demurely outside his door, dressed in what Mary surmises is her version of conservative: a hot pink suit with a plunging neckline and micro-mini skirt, six-inch stiletto heels, heavy gold chains and bracelets, extreme makeup, and of course, Rumplesnakeskin in plain sight.

The interview process has undergone dramatic changes in the last 20 years. Today, every candidate is expected to be tech savvy, to have a strong social media presence and an unassailable "digital footprint," and of course, to have the education and experience to do the job. These attributes are essential, but what employers value most are well-honed interpersonal skills.

Social Skills

Fresh out of Bates College, one of the most highly regarded liberal arts schools in New England, 23-year-old psychology major Tully knew how fortunate he was to be offered a personal recommendation for a job at a top software company. This got him in the door. The rest was up to him.

On the day of the interview, Tully groomed himself impeccably from head to toe and dressed in what he called his best "techie attire": a plaid shirt, pressed khakis, and brown loafers. Tully spent the next six hours in meetings with a HR rep, a team leader, and team members, all of whom would offer input on his candidacy. He was told he would hear from them that afternoon. Tully went home feeling hopeful and waited. Two hours later, he got the call—and the job.

How did he do it? Tully had done his research, boning up on the company's culture and the position he sought. He found common areas of interest with his interviewers, talking about his recent travels to Thailand and Greece, his fascination with nature photography, and his love of running. Tully attributed his success to his ability to successfully establish rapport. His interviewers warmed to him because he himself is a genuinely warm person.

Just how important are social skills? Tom Malone of MIT's Center for Collective Intelligence says, "It is becoming increasingly important to think about business and organizations not just in terms of how efficient or how productive they are, but also how intelligent they are."[1] When Mr. Malone conducted research, he found that just having "a bunch of smart people in a group" does not necessarily make for a smart group. What *does* make a group smart is the average social perceptiveness of the group members.

Employers agree. In its article "15 Traits of the Ideal Employee," *Forbes* states, "The most intelligent companies hire on future success and heavily weigh personality when determining the most apt employees."[2] Of course, most employers *do* look for technical skills as well, but depending upon the job, not having them is not necessarily a deal breaker. Even in a workplace that demands the ability to master tech tools, many employers are hiring for attitude and training for skill. They have found that you can teach technology but it is far more difficult, if not impossible, to instill in individuals the critical qualities of patience, kindness, and empathy.

Many hiring managers say that they know within a minute or two whether or not they will hire someone. Immediate red flags are candidates who are late, inappropriately dressed, do not make eye contact, or leave their cell phones on and out. Once a conversation is underway, a candidate who knows nothing about the company's culture, is too focused on himself, or disparages a previous employer is disqualified as well.

In her *Business Insider* article, "The All-Time Worst Interview Mistakes Job Candidates Have Made," Vivian Giang writes of the applicant who warned the interviewer that she had probably taken too much Valium that day, the one who asked for a hug before the interview began, and the one who pretended he was getting a call from the interviewer's competitor. The applicant who asked for the phone number of the company's receptionist because he really liked her also made the list.[3]

The Hiring Process

It's been 30 years since Bob, a business service consultant, has looked for a job. Bob has worked at the same telecommunications company for his entire career, and he knows the job search and interview processes have changed dramatically in those 30 years. Now that his office has moved out of state, he is about to find out just how much. The first thing he does is call the local competitor, where he wanders through a maze of telephone options. He finally reaches a live human voice in HR and is promptly told that they do not field employment inquiries. All information about available jobs and application instructions would be on their website.

It was on the website that he sees what he is up against. Bob would first be asked to register, complete a detailed online application, and attach a current résumé with references. Next, he would need to take a two-hour three-part pre-assessment test to determine his technical ability, behavioral profile, and problem-solving acumen. If he met all of the requirements, he would then be contacted for a telephone-screening interview. If all went well and he was selected for an in-person interview, he would first meet with a hiring manager. Any subsequent interviews would involve meetings with company representatives at various levels, as well as presentations and role-playing exercises. If he were to be offered a job, he would then submit to an extensive background check.

Bob sighs. He knew he had his work cut out for him in getting a job, but he didn't know how much of a job it would be just to get through the interview process.

Job seekers who have been out of the market for any length of time are in for a big surprise. The scenario of "mail in your résumé and wait by the phone" has long since been replaced by technology. Indeed, Luddites, those opposed to technology, need not apply. Even though the majority of jobs are still found through networking and internal opportunities, not online, one still needs at least a baseline of tech ability to apply. Companies typically require an online application to even begin the process and candidates' social media will likely be vetted.

Social media is a double-edged sword for job candidates. They must have a social media presence, especially on LinkedIn, but anything discovered and deemed inappropriate can be held against them. This can be a big problem for digital natives, as online sharing is just what they do. John Challenger of Challenger, Gray & Christmas, offers some hope to those who have ever made a misstep online. "There is more understanding of these communications tools, as well as the realization that if you eliminate every candidate with problematic Facebook or Twitter posts, you would quickly run out of candidates,"[4] he says. But counting on a stranger to generously overlook an online misstep is a risky strategy, especially if there is a lot of competition for the job.

Employers go deep in their research. They begin with Google, going back several pages to see what is in a person's background. Then they move on to Facebook to get a sense of the candidate's personality and attitude. They look at pictures but also read posts to understand the tone with which the person interacts with friends. Does she come across as positive, encouraging, even funny, or is there a drumbeat of negativity? The person's grammar and spelling are noted and judged. The employer begins to form an overall impression of a candidate—her intelligence, judgment, and character—all before they even meet.

A check of Twitter comes next. Here, recruiters first want to see if candidates are on the platform, and if they are, exactly what they are doing. Are they tweeting and re-tweeting relevant information? Are they sharing interesting articles and helpful links? Are they following thought and industry leaders? Are they promoting professional affiliations and memberships? Or are they recounting the mundane details of their daily lives? Answers to these questions help recruiters gauge a candidate's level of seriousness and provide additional character clues. From there, recruiters move on to LinkedIn to view candidates' executive summaries, references, and industry memberships. Finally, they check YouTube.

What else are companies doing to identify and vet candidates? More and more, they are relying upon big data, a term that refers to the vast amount of information now available from a multitude of seemingly disparate sources. Gill Press, a contributor to *Fortune/Tech,* says big data is "a new attitude by businesses, non-profits, government agencies, and individuals that combining data from multiple sources could lead to better decisions."[5] "Big data is fast becoming a vital component of the modern Human Resources toolkit and the advantages go far beyond the ability to identify the brightest and best talent,"[6] reports Orlaith Finnegan of Digimind Insights, a social intelligence blog. Companies are now retaining firms like Entelo and Talent Bin to help them in the recruiting process. These, and other organizations, not only analyze prospective candidates' activity on social media platforms, but also on other sites specific to their fields.

Employers may also be factoring in Klout Scores, a ranking of 1–100 by which online social influence is measured using social media analytics. Klout scores are determined by the amount of engagement people generate from their use of social media based upon the amount of content they share. In his article entitled "Does Your Klout Score Matter?" James A. Martin quotes Ron Culp, instructor and professional director of the Public Relations and Advertising (MA) Program at DePaul University College of Communication. Mr. Culp says, "Klout matters big time to hiring managers, often serving as a tie breaker in hiring decisions involving two equally solid candidates."[7] Not everyone agrees about how important Klout scores are to hiring managers, but candidates must be prepared for the fact that their scores could matter.

PREPARATION

- **Conduct a social media audit.** Review everything that you and others have posted, going back years. Take down posts that reflect poorly on you, and ask others to do the same. Remove photos of drinking, drug use, offensive activities or gestures, or inappropriate clothing. Remove posts that include profanity, intolerant views, or unethical behavior, and those of a political, religious, or very personal nature.
- **Be judicious with future posts.** Refrain from putting anything online that could hurt your job prospects in the future.
- **Block or remove friends and connections, if necessary.** Do not allow others' posts to possibly reflect negatively upon you.

LinkedIn is considered the primary platform for professional networking, but savvy job seekers do not overlook Facebook. With some 1.71 *billion* monthly users at this writing and at roughly four times the size of LinkedIn, Facebook has become a major job search tool. Using Facebook to your best advantage means first completing the section on work and education. Next, organize your connections to create lists of professionals with whom you want to share work-search updates. Use search bars to find out who among your connections work at certain companies, and stay active by posting relevant articles, liking connections' posts, and liking target companies' pages.

On LinkedIn, make sure you have completed your profile and are a member of relevant industry groups. Post thoughtfully at appropriate intervals. To help recruiters find you, use keywords in your profile and branding statement. Avail yourself of the numerous online tools and sites available for job seekers.

The Interview Experience

When Ginger congratulated Scott, one of her LinkedIn connections, on his new job, she had no idea how important this relationship would become. A few months later, after a company downsizing, the 55-year-old HR executive became unemployed herself. She was now in the job market and needed the network she had nurtured to help her. Scott, the LinkedIn connection she had congratulated, now had a job lead for her! Three months and 13 in-person interviews later, Ginger got great news. She would once again be employed as an HR executive!

Ginger accomplished this by paying careful attention to detail. She did in-depth company research, videotaped herself in practice interviews, and prepared an extensive list of thoughtful questions. She dressed for the conservative culture in which she hoped to work, wearing tailored suits and dresses, understated jewelry and makeup, hosiery, and appropriate shoes. She carried her résumé in a black leather portfolio and made sure she had two elegant working pens. When introducing herself and shaking hands, she made sure her name badge was placed on her right, in the direct line of vision of the person she was meeting. In the interview room, Ginger waited to be offered a seat, asked if she could take notes, maintained eye contact, asked salient questions, mirrored her interviewer's tone of voice and facial expressions, and was respectful of any time constraints. She sent a personal thank-you email after every meeting or conversation.

After the interview process was completed, Ginger followed up at weekly intervals. She did *not* ask about compensation, vacation time, or benefits until after the job was offered. It all paid off to ensure her final success.

Debbie Monosson, president of Boston Financial and Equity, a capital equipment leasing company, describes her interview process. She starts by placing ads on LinkedIn and in college career centers. She then contacts interested candidates by email, asking them to respond with short paragraphs about why they want the position. The professionalism of their responses determines whether they are invited in for in-person interviews. The candidate who wrote back asking if she would remind him of what the position was did not get an invitation to interview. There are deal breakers during the interview, as well. The candidate who showed up wearing chinos and a T-shirt was not offered a job, nor was the one who put his cell phone on the table. "It vibrated. To his credit, he did not answer the phone," Ms. Monosson said. But just having it out, and the interruption it caused, cost him the job offer. When an interview goes really well, however, she says she often offers a job on the spot.

Today's interview process often starts with an online application. A telephone screening call may come next, followed by a Skype interview and anywhere from one to a dozen or more one-on-one and/or team interviews. Depending upon the position, interviews may include behavior-based questions to see how candidates handled specific challenges, and questions about their decision-making and problem-solving processes. They may also be asked about their communication and management styles and their goals for the future. They will certainly be asked what they know about the company and the position, why they want to work there, and what they will contribute. They will be asked about their employment and educational backgrounds, their salary expectations, and what questions they have for the interviewer. A request for a presentation or completion of an assignment may also be part of the process.

Even after a job offer is made and accepted, a candidate cannot relax just yet. She may be subjected to a complete background check including credit reports, criminal records, bankruptcies, military service, worker's compensation claims, and some medical records. Employers may check education, certifications, licenses, salary history, job history, and driving records. Drug testing may also be part of the process, and references from former employers may be requested.

Résumés and Cover Letters

Well-written résumés and cover letters are still necessary even when online applications are required. Regardless of the position, a résumé needs to be organized, concise, and easy to read, with perfect spelling and grammar. It also needs to be attention grabbing and compelling enough to get more than a cursory glance. A typical hiring manager sifts through dozens of résumés at a time and may spend just seconds looking at any one résumé.

There are many serviceable boilerplate résumé and cover letter examples from which to choose, but it is important to avoid writing anything that looks formulaic or that could be used for a variety of positions. You will also want to research firms and fine-tune your résumé and cover letter so that your experience and skills align with what the employer seeks.

It is useful to note that hiring managers are increasingly using technology to help them sift through their databases of résumés. Incorporate keywords from their job ads into your résumé to increase the odds of having yours read. You may decide that a career coach and a professionally written résumé are excellent investments of time and money.

The Job Search

Although the majority of jobs seekers today still find jobs through networking and internal opportunities, many are going online in their searches. To keep private information out of the wrong hands, avoid posting a résumé on a job board, and send it directly to the hiring manager. You can also use job-site privacy settings and a temporary phone number or address for the duration of your job search.

Searching for a job is a full-time job, which can be problematic for someone already employed. But a well thought out approach will help you stay organized.

- **Networks.** Include every contact you have ever made personally, professionally, and through social media.
- **Internet and social media.** Create a blog through free blogging services, such as Google's blogger.com. Use of a résumé distribution service may also be helpful.
- **Job boards.** Use advanced search options available on all major sites, including monster.com, careerbuilder.com, indeed.com, and simplyhired.com.

- **Goals.** Establish job search goals and keep detailed notes. Use a spreadsheet for keeping track of applications made, persons contacted, dates interviewed, correspondence sent, follow-up dates, and additional companies and individuals to contact.

Telephone Interviews

Being contacted for a telephone interview indicates that you have made it through the preliminary screening process. Usually conducted by an HR representative, it is used to determine whether or not an in-person interview with a hiring manager is in order. During a telephone interview, which usually lasts about 30 minutes, your demeanor, confidence, and verbal communication style are noted and evaluated. The interviewer's task is to ascertain enough basic information to make a decision about whether to recommend you for an in-person interview. It is critically important that you consider this conversation the most important one in the process. All subsequent interviews depend on its success.

When preparing for a telephone interview, select an environment that is conducive to a business conversation. This means controlling potential distractions, such as noisy electronic devices, and ensuring family members, roommates, and dogs are out of the room. Additionally, plan to hold the conversation in a private place and never while walking or driving. If possible, use a landline instead of a mobile phone. A dropped call or tenuous connection will impact the flow of the conversation and potentially affect your confidence and concentration.

Do your homework and prepare good questions about the job and how you can help the organization. Allow the interviewer to lead the conversation. Be prepared to talk through your résumé in detail. Answer all questions truthfully, even if they are about potentially tricky topics such as gaps in employment or job change frequency. Do not ask about salary, vacation, or start date at this point.

Your tone of voice will account for 70 percent of the message you convey on the telephone. Be energetic and humorous, if appropriate, and smile! The interviewer will not see your smile, but it will come through. Take time to answer questions thoughtfully, but do not worry if you do not have time to say everything you would like. If all goes well, you will soon have that opportunity at an in-person interview.

At the conclusion of the call, thank the interviewer for her time. If you are interested in pursuing this opportunity, follow-up with an email relating your qualifications to the job requirements and expressing your continued interest in the position.

Skype Interviews

The Skype interview, or one conducted via Voice over Internet Protocol (VoIP), has many similarities to the telephone interview. But of course, on Skype, they can see you! This will require extra preparation to be sure you are appropriately groomed and attired and that the physical space in which you are sitting is appropriate as well. Sit in front of a neutral background with no distracting photos or decorations behind you. Maintain eye contact with the interviewer by looking at the camera, and not at yourself on the screen. Sit up straight, keep gestures to a minimum, and keep your hands away from your face and hair. Nods of understanding and smiling as appropriate are great, but try not to frown or show displeasure. Practice a Skype interview beforehand with a friend. You want no glitches on the big day!

In-Person Interviews

At an in-person interview, you are evaluated by a whole new set of criteria. Your interviewer is trying to get a sense of you as a whole person, not just a list of academic achievements and skill sets. He immediately notices your attire and grooming, whether you are late, even by a minute (or too early), how you introduce yourself and shake hands, the degree of respect in your tone, your eye contact and facial expressions, and your standing and seated posture.

Once the conversation is underway, your attitude, enthusiasm, engagement, and level of preparedness are now all on display. You are judged on how well you listen, the questions you ask, and whether your focus is upon your needs rather than upon how you can add value within the organization. No two interviewers are alike in their styles or in the kinds of questions they ask, but all know a respectful, prepared, and confident candidate when they meet one. You can show your preparedness by researching beforehand on glassdoor.com to learn about a specific company's interview process, or by visiting readyprepinterview.com for the interview questions most often asked for this job.

Candidates should be prepared for unusual questions. Ostensibly used to determine how quickly and creatively candidates think on their feet and how well they deal with stress, the practice of purposely asking difficult or unanswerable questions is questionable in my opinion. But if candidates are faced with such questions, the best they can do is deflect the questions with humor and keep calm! Some real-life examples from glassdoor.com:

- "Using a scale of 1–10, rate yourself on how weird you are." —*Capital One*
- "How many bricks are there in Shanghai? Consider only residential buildings." —*Deloitte Consulting*
- "You are in charge of 20 people. Organize them to find out how many bicycles were sold in your area last year." —*Schlumberger*
- "What's your fastball?" —*Ernst & Young*[8]

If, after the interview, you would still like to be considered for the position, send an email that day to thank the interviewer and to reiterate your interest and the strength of your candidacy. Follow up no more than once weekly or as directed by the interviewer. Perhaps the most difficult, but most critical, aspect of the interview process is exhibiting patience. Enthusiasm and interest work in your favor; a sense that you are desperate does not.

After all of your hard work, you've gotten the job. Congratulations! What are you going to do first? Share your great news with everyone who helped you. Whether they provided advice, introductions, encouragement, or assistance, let them know how grateful you are and that you would welcome the chance to be of help to them in some way in the future.

At this point, it is also considered good form, and good strategy, to let other prospective employers know you have accepted a job offer. Thank them for their interest, and tell them how much you enjoyed meeting them and how impressed you were with their organizations. This will allow them to keep their lists of viable applicants current and distinguish you as a considerate job candidate.

There is a chance you will receive job offers you choose not to accept. Handle such situations with the same gratitude, grace, and tact. You need not get too specific, such as saying you did not like someone you had met or that you thought the company was subpar. If pressed, just say the fit wasn't quite right for you. And always keep your eyes on the future. In her 2015 article *in Business Insider,* Jacquelyn Smith says, "The business world, your industry and market are all small. Your hiring manager can likely reappear in your career. So put your best foot forward, especially when you refuse a position."[9]

There is always the *remote* possibility that despite your very best efforts, you did not win the position. Clearly, this is a difficult situation, especially if you were one of the finalists. But, believe it or not, the way in which you handle this "rejection" may actually end up working in your favor. First, try to see all the good that came of this process. You met new people, got to hone your interview skills, and learned more about the requirements for the position. And to get as far as you did, you obviously impressed a lot of people. Now it's time to cement their good impressions.

Start by thanking everyone who interviewed you. Let them know that you would still be very interested in joining the organization should another opportunity arise. Ask for feedback about why they selected another candidate and how you could possibly improve your technical or interview skills. Candid feedback is not always easy to get, but a recruiter may be willing to do this. Ask if you can stay in touch from time to time, and assuming the answer is yes, do so by forwarding relevant articles, offering congratulations for good news, and recommending candidates who you think could help them.

All of this may come back to help you sooner than you think. If you came in second place, and the job is either not accepted or does not work out for the first-place candidate, you will be the first person they call. Interviewers will be far more likely to recommend a gracious candidate to their networks than one who seemed to sulk, or worse, badmouthed a prospective employer because she did not get the job. Remember, your brand is always on display. How you handle disappointment tells others a great deal about your character, professionalism, resilience, and maturity.

The Generational Challenge

The interview seems to be going really well for recent grad Alex. He thinks he may be offered the job, as the hiring manager is now describing the next steps. With a big smile, the interviewer asks Alex if he has any questions. "Just one," says Alex. "What's your lead time for drug testing?" That's when the smile froze.

Most job search challenges are faced equally by candidates of all ages. But there are some generation-specific challenges with which candidates might need to contend, challenges often fueled by stereotypes. For example, millennials may have to combat the notion that they all feel "entitled," and baby boomers that they are all "over the hill." Here is some advice on what the generations can do to challenge any preconceived notions or age-related speed bumps they may encounter.

Digital Natives

Millennials, you are not in charge—yet. But you soon will be. And as long as you alone create the code, don't you own the marketplace? Perhaps ... *if* tech skills were all one needed to succeed. But this is not now nor will it ever be the case. Even if it were the case, millennials would not have a corner on technical expertise for much longer. Generation Z is coming up fast. The oldest of this cohort of true digital natives are now around 20 years of age. As they begin to enter the workplace, technical skills will no longer be the exclusive domain of millennials, and social skills will once again become the distinguishing commodity.

Fairly or unfairly, Gen Y has been painted as a socially clueless cohort. In his article for Monster.com, "How to Help Millennials Fill the Soft Skills Gap," John Rossheim wrote, "Gen Y employees, raised to believe that hard skills matter most, often fall short on soft skills." He adds, "The soft skill gaps most likely to trip up millennials include written and oral communications, social skills and the ability to engage and motivate, business etiquette, and professionalism."[10] In her article "Just Look Me in the Eye Already," Sue Shellenbarger of *the Wall Street Journal* puts an even finer point on the challenges this group faces. "Eye contact, so vital an element of respect among preceding generations, seems conspicuously missing from millennials."[11]

As a millennial job candidate, you can overcome these preconceptions by realizing that interviewers are on the lookout for such stereotypical behavior. They've also done additional homework. They know that technology is part of your DNA. They know of the social conscience you embody as a group, the flexible work-life balance you seek, the feedback you crave, the aspirations you have for fast and continuous development and advancement, the casual work environment you prefer, and yes, your interest in food, food, and more food! All of these are things you do not need to tell them. Your fellow Gen Ys will ask about job perks, gym memberships, office decor allowances, bringing their dogs to work, and using company equipment for their new start-ups. Those are their issues. Just be sure they are not yours.

Why *shouldn't* candidates announce their clear wishes from the get-go? Because employers who are seriously interested in them will not only be willing to share the many benefits their companies offer, they will be shouting these benefits from the rooftops. Applicants of all ages need to guard against thinking that they are more important to their prospective employers than the employers are to them. It is only after a job offer is made that a candidate is in any position of strength.

The good news for millennials is that they do not have to do much to tip the employment scales in their favor. If their education and experience match their prospective employers' needs, brushing up on such social skills such as small talk, eye contact, handshakes, and turning devices *off* may be all that's required to get the jobs.

Digital Immigrants

Older job applicants face their share of challenges in the interview process as well, starting with who interviews them. Anyone in the job market who is *not* a millennial is almost certainly going to be interviewed *by* one at some point during the process. This means trying to impress a potential boss some 20 or 30 years one's junior.

Applicants interviewing with millennials will want to keep in mind the defining characteristics of this generation. Applicants should speak to what millennials value most: work-life integration, teamwork, and continuous learning. They should offer positive feedback to interviewers on their questions and insights and keep focus squarely on the present and future, not on the past.

Albert Einstein once said, "Learning is not a product of schooling but the lifelong attempt to acquire it." Older applicants know they need to stay current with technology, but wonder how they can when it moves at the speed of light. The answer is through education, in whatever form they can find it. Community college and online courses, YouTube videos, paid seminars, free classes, and reverse mentoring with younger colleagues, children, grandchildren, and neighbors can all provide excellent low-cost or no-cost sources of up-to-the-minute information. Older workers should not be afraid to ask for help. They have so much of value to offer in return—college referral letters, key introductions, and free room and board among them!

Despite proof to the contrary, older workers suffer from misconceptions about their energy, stamina, productivity, and adaptability. To keep age from being your defining characteristic, Carmine P. Gibaldi, Professor of Organizational Behavior and Management at St. John's University and Harvard University, advises working late one or two nights each week, letting co-workers know you exercise, keeping current with your clothing, and staying positive. He also recommends not talking about how things used to be done, not advertising your lack of tech savvy, and not complaining about your bad back![12] Older candidates and employees also want to make sure that 21st century tech-speak and skills are part of their repertoires.

REMEMBER

- Master the use of technology for job searches and interviews.
- Learn the interview requirements of a particular job or field.
- Develop and nurture networks.
- Stay organized and follow up meticulously.

chapter 3

professional presence

Getting It Right

"Your manners are always under examination, and by committees little suspected, awarding or denying you very high prizes when you least think of it."

—RALPH WALDO EMERSON

Gen Xer Joe doesn't know when his alarm clock buzzes for the second time how much his job will be on the line later that morning. Now, with his heart pounding wildly, he is in full panic mode. Joe's new district manager is visiting this morning and will be addressing rumors about a possible company downsizing. Joe knows he had better get to the office before the DM does.

Joe grabs the pile of clothes lying on the floor, the same ones he had worn the day before, and after a quick sniff test, wildly pulls them on. He brushes his teeth and drags a comb through his hair before he is out the door.

Joe has a lot of time to make up and his foot is heavy on the gas. Weaving in and out of traffic, he gets pulled over. Politely accepting his speeding ticket, Joe is now desperate to get to work. At the company parking lot, he barely misses the car stopped at the front entrance. He blares his horn as a passenger leaves the car and slowly walks to the entrance. Joe finally parks and rushes into the building. He dashes up the stairs into the meeting room disheveled, breathless, dripping in sweat, and two minutes late.

His boss and coworkers stare at him in disbelief. And then, the man at the far end of the conference table stands, and Joe and the district manager lock eyes in mutual recognition. Here is the passenger of the car stopped at the entrance, the very same car at which Joe had blared his horn. And he looks very unhappy. Joe sinks into the nearest seat, head bowed, and prepares for the worst.

If you've ever wondered if you have a personal brand, wonder no more. You do. We all do. Where we live, what we drive, with whom we associate, what we wear, how we communicate both in person and virtually, our work habits, and our leisure activities combine to create an indelible image and powerful message. Who we are and what we value, in essence, define our personal brands. Your personal brand precedes you and stays long after you have left. Says Jeff Bezos, CEO of Amazon, "Your brand is what people say about you when you are not in the room."

The Right Brand

It has been almost a month to the day since Karen, a 33-year-old CPA at a major accounting firm, has taken her "voluntary" Professional Presence training. Indisputably brilliant at her job, Karen has rapidly worked her way up from staff auditor to tax manager and is on track to become one of the firm's youngest partners. That is, *if* she is able to convince the senior partners that she can project the image they have so carefully developed for their firm.

Karen knows she can be a little rough around the edges. Impatient and demanding, she is a perfectionist. After all, time is money—her clients' and the firm's—and she's not going to waste any of it. Still, her salty language, severe attire, and unsmiling face intimidate the junior staff and even put off some of the partners, as well. But this is who she is, Karen thinks, an accountant, not a cruise director. Besides, a "lipstick" approach to changing her image will never work.

Karen had no choice but to take the training if she wanted to become partner—which she desperately did. But she was skeptical when the consultant said that little tweaks could actually make big differences. If Karen was willing to make a few changes, she said, she might be pleasantly surprised at how powerful the effects could be. They would meet again in a month to assess her progress.

Karen figured she had nothing to lose. She made an appointment with a personal shopper and a hair salon to update her wardrobe and hairstyle. She visited a cosmetics counter and was astonished at what a difference a little well-applied makeup made. At work, Karen began greeting colleagues as they passed by and was surprised when her greetings were invariably returned. Rather than her usual all-business approach, she engaged her staff in light conversations about their weekend plans and outside interests, and truly listened to their responses. She even invited some coworkers to coffee—something she'd never done in the past—and began to forge some new relationships. She was amazed at how receptive people were. But the biggest shock for Karen was that she had begun to receive compliments about her appearance and attitude—that was a first!

Karen's confidence was sky-high, and she had to acknowledge her new approach wasn't hurting her team's productivity at all—in fact, it actually seemed to be helping it. Karen looked forward to her follow-up meeting with the consultant, eager to share her successes and to ask for additional tips. All of a sudden, her partnership dream seemed very much within her grasp.

The concept of brands is not new. First introduced in 1937 by Napoleon Hill in his book *Think and Grow Rich*,[1] personal branding was again brought to the fore in 1981 by Al Ries and Jack Trout in their book *Positioning: The Battle for Your Mind*.[2] It was later popularized by management guru Tom Peters in his 1997 article in *Fast Company*, "A Brand Called You."[3]

Professional image and reputation have always been important. But there is a new sense of urgency in having a positive brand, due to the proliferation of social media. In the past, the implications of a person's brand, whether good or bad, were largely contained. Only specific family, work, and community audiences were privy to them. Today, the possible ramifications of a negative brand are enormous because everything is out there for the whole world to see.

Occasionally, personal branding suffers from a negative connotation. When less than truthful self-promotion reveals itself, a letdown inevitably occurs. Conversely, while openness is to be valued where matters of character are concerned, sharing too much information can work against you. Today's workplace mantra is "transparency and authenticity," but the fact is, true civility requires good judgment and a measure of nondisclosure.

It is easier than ever to inflict permanent damage to our brands. We would be wise to heed the advice of Guru Sai Baba, who said, "Before you speak, ask yourself: is it kind, is it necessary, is it true, does it improve on the silence?" If what we are about to say does not meet these criteria, it may be better left unsaid.

Dan Schawbel, author of *Personal Branding Book,* says personal branding is "The process by which individuals differentiate themselves and stand out from a crowd by identifying their unique value proposition, whether professional or personal, and then leveraging it across platforms with a consistent message to achieve a specific goal."[4] The benefits of having a strong personal brand, he says, include the ability to demand a premium price, a higher salary, and enhanced visibility within professional communities.

One's in-person persona and online activities combine to create a brand—a brand that can easily be compromised. Online, a brand can be undermined by one's failure to include a professional photograph, poor judgment with posts, relentless self-promoting, and over-sharing. In person, it can be marred by behaviors at work, on public transportation, in restaurants, on elevators, while waiting in line, and while walking on the sidewalk or into buildings—virtually anyplace one is seen or heard.

Perceptions of people are also fueled by stereotypes. If one wishes to overcome the preconceived notions that millennials are flighty narcissists and baby boomers are cranky has-beens, one will need to build an authentic, compelling personal brand that flies in the face of these stereotypes. To accomplish this, deliberation is key, and it begins with self-reflection. Brian Lawrence, a career development specialist at Saint Louis University, says that a personal brand is first and foremost *personal.* "Your brand should not be a character you create but instead should be a representation of what employers can expect when you are hired."[5] Once you determine who you are and what you want to convey, you can align all aspects of your personal and professional personas and begin to clearly and consistently communicate your brand.

Sometimes *rebranding* is in order. One of the most famous comeback stories is that of Steve Jobs. He founded Apple in 1976, got kicked out of the company in 1985, and 12 years later was rehired. Henry Blodget, cofounder and former CEO of the business website businessinsider.com, wrote, "During his time in the wilderness—the 12 years he spent away from the company that became his life's work—Steve learned the skills and discipline that he needed to lead Apple's resurrection. Steven wasn't born with these skills, he *developed* them."[6] Bill Gates and Richard Branson, among others, also faced significant setbacks in their careers. What is encouraging is that no matter how great the challenge or how long it takes, rebranding is not only possible, it may land one in a far better position than before.

The newly hired are at an advantage because they are in the process of making their first impressions. They can turn these good impressions into good brands. Tenured employees, on the other hand, or those who have made less than positive first impressions, may need to do some rebranding. This involves first convincing themselves, and then others, that they are not only capable of making successful changes, but also would thrive in doing so.

SUCCESSFUL REBRANDING

- **Take seriously all feedback received.** Make personal improvements with an eye toward the future.
- **Determine how current skills align with future job requirements.** Learn necessary skills for a new job before pursuing it. Find mentors to lend support and give advice.
- **Realize rebranding takes time.** Be persistent and confident. Eventually, others will change their minds about you and your capabilities.

The Right Attitude

Helen approaches Tom, the new manager of the regional office. "Do you have a minute?" she asks. Eager to assist, Tom invites her in to his office. With a worried look on her face, Helen, one of the company's sales assistants, begins. "I am hesitant to say this, but as the new manager, you have a right to know. And I really just want to help." Helen now has Tom's full attention.

"Unfortunately, we have some big problems on our team." In a voice full of concern, Helen reports that Tina's difficult home life is affecting her attendance, Brett's drinking problem makes him late most days, Jeff's money woes are making him miserable to be around, and Susan's poor performance is because she can't get along with her clients. "Rich's behavior is the most problematic, though," Helen says with great drama. "Now that his marriage is on the rocks, he's beginning to hit on all the young female interns."

After she finishes describing virtually every person on the team in an unflattering, personal way, Helen sighs heavily, a barely perceptible look of smugness on her face. Tom thinks for a moment and says, "You're right, Helen, we do have a problem. It's your attitude. What are you going to do about that?"

The importance of a positive attitude cannot be overstated. In his article, "The One Thing That Determines How Successful You Can Be," author Jim Rohn says attitude "determines the level of our potential, produces the intensity of our activity, and predicts the quality of the result we receive."[7] Charles Swindoll, pastor and author, says attitude is a greater determinant of future success than one's background, education, financial means, position, or reputation with others. He says attitude is more important than the past, the future, and even the facts.[8]

Still, bad attitudes on the job run rampant, and those who have them run the gamut. From the complainer, the victim, and the martyr to the self-proclaimed overworked, under-paid, and under-appreciated, these individuals share and often over-share their feelings, about, well, everything. Nothing is off the table: relationships, politics, ill-health, weather, traffic, long lines, discourteous commuters, bosses, coworkers, work conditions, job loads, paychecks, deadlines—the list is endless. On the job, bad attitudes are evidenced by tardiness, rudeness, gossip, poor work habits, inappropriate attire, and negative tones. They are also demonstrated through disrespectful nonverbal communication such as slouching, eye rolling, glaring, smirking, and the use of electronic devices.

There are myriad reasons people exhibit bad attitudes, including to get attention, avoid responsibility, achieve common ground, and gain validation. Fear, insecurity, jealousy, and bad habits are also factors that lead to negative attitudes. And blameless colleagues, unsuspecting customers, and innocent business partners all take the hit.

Of course, there are issues of legitimate concern that can affect attitudes, including serious health, family, and money matters. And there are generation-specific concerns as well. Digital natives in particular are worried. While the current national unemployment rate of 5 percent means many are landing jobs, they still carry an average of $37,000 in school loan debt alone.[9] According to the Census Bureau, some 30 percent of young adults aged 18–34 are living with their parents,[10] creating a challenging "full nest" situation for parents and their adult children. At an age where thoughts traditionally turn to establishing relationships, buying homes, and starting families, such considerations are on the back burner for many millennials. This lack of money and independence contribute to a high degree of stress for many in this cohort. Digital immigrants also have a lot on their minds as retirement security, health and healthcare, employment security, children's educations, and the needs of aging parents weigh heavily.

Regardless of the challenge, it is still our responsibility to choose the right attitudes, because the alternative is just too costly. Negative attitudes have deleterious effects on physical and emotional health. They drain energy, weaken immune systems, contribute to depression, lengthen illness recovery times, and shorten life. Negative attitudes at work decrease productivity, lower morale, overshadow accomplishments, damage relationships, and jeopardize business, jobs, and promotions. Bad attitudes permeate corporate cultures from top to bottom.

Positive attitudes, on the other hand, provide enormous benefits. They engender respect, encourage the perceptions of confidence, strength, and leadership ability, facilitate optimum job productivity and satisfaction, and promote strong professional relationships.

You can become a member of the "positive attitude club" with a few simple steps. First, do a gut check by acknowledging your feelings and recognizing how you are broadcasting them. Ask yourself whether an issue will matter tomorrow, next month, or five years from now. If the answer is no, let it go. Improve the situation if you can, but be prepared to move on in a healthy way when there's nothing more you can do.

With coworkers, demonstrate your good attitude by treating everyone with respect and kindness. Use positive language, banishing words like *problem* and *impossible* from your lexicon. Offer compliments, encouragement, congratulations, and apologies as warranted. Show optimism and appreciation. Go above and beyond, without expectation of recognition. In addition to doing your part in creating a positive work environment, all of these efforts can reap you great personal and professional rewards.

Now that you've put on the right attitude for work, it's time to put on the right clothes!

The Right Appearance

After a career that spanned nearly five decades, Walter, a 74-year-old financial advisor at one of the country's largest wealth management companies, was about to retire. But before he did, this very successful man needed to devise a succession plan for his longstanding clients, many of whom were high net-worth individuals in their 60s, 70s, and above. They trusted him completely, and Walter knew the importance of this last business decision for his clients—and for his legacy. He was not going to let them down.

Walter had a dozen or more skilled advisors in the office to whom he could pass his clients, and all of the advisors were technically proficient and would do a fine job. But in the end, he chose 35-year-old Patrick. Walter's final decision was influenced not only by Patrick's overall professionalism, but very much by the way Patrick dressed. His clients still respected formal business attire, including shined shoes, pressed suits, and "neckties," as they called them. Walter was confident that his clients would feel very comfortable being transferred to Patrick and that the company had an excellent chance of retaining their business for years to come. A career's worth of valuable contacts and business went to Patrick, because he "dressed the part."

Attire is a big part of one's personal brand. Attire tells the world what one thinks about oneself and others. It conveys competence and judgment, or the lack thereof. It inspires confidence or elicits concern. It enhances credibility or creates confusion. It matters. Attire is the first thing others notice at an interview and on the job. It can be a deciding factor between the person who gets the job, the client, or the promotion and the person who does not. Dressing professionally is not about the latest styles or comfort. It is about reflecting and supporting a specific workplace culture and industry standards by meeting expectations, not defying them.

It is often argued that attire, as mere "packaging," is not important. It's what's inside that counts. But in order to entice others to be interested in what's inside, they must be intrigued— or at least not put off—by what's outside. The importance of packaging was reinforced for me daily during my 11 years working in the business sales division of Tiffany & Co. Known for its trademark "little blue box," the venerable jeweler has never lost sight of the power of its packaging and goes to great lengths to defend infringement upon its brand. On occasions when I was asked if I could supply a Tiffany box, I would always say yes, as long as it contained paid-for Tiffany merchandise. I understood the assumptions made about this packaging. The mere sight of a Tiffany blue box held a promise, if not a guarantee, that whatever was inside was of unsurpassed beauty and quality. Attire, or one's packaging, has similar power.

Digital immigrants remember well when there was no question about what to wear to work: for men, it was a suit and tie, and for women, it was a dress (or skirt and blouse) and hosiery. Today, these standards have been relaxed dramatically, even in the most staid environments. Whether this is a good thing is under debate. In his *Financial Times* article, "Sorry, JP Morgan, Smart Guys Still Wear Suits," Robert Armstrong took issue with the announcement by the world's leading bank urging its employees to adopt business casual attire. Among Mr. Armstrong's arguments against this standard of attire was "Put a suit on, hotshot, it's other people's money."[11]

In deciding what to wear, the culture of the organization is always the major determining factor. There is no "one size fits all." Even within a corporate culture, there may be different or relaxed standards depending upon the physical location of an office or what a person does for an organization. Expectations for attire at corporate headquarters where executives and important clients roam may be different from dress standards in field offices; warmer climates may dictate lighter fabrics and fewer items of clothing; regional standards of dress in a conservative Northeast work environment may be different from a laid-back West Coast concern.

We dress to meet expectations—not to cause confusion or concern. A uniformed police officer, firefighter, or nurse reassures us that a professional is on the scene. A hard-hatted construction worker or white-coated scientist suggests someone who respects and is prepared for the job. A suited and buttoned-down accountant or banker instills confidence in us that good care will be taken with our money. In an operating room, you hope the surgeon is wearing scrubs; in a court of law, you hope the judge is wearing black robes.

What you wear depends on what you do and where you do it. If you work in a conservative field such as law or financial services, conservative attire is the way to go. If you're in a creative field, such as marketing or advertising, dressing in an *avant-garde* style is in order. Hoodies are often the uniform of the day in the high-tech field, and the fashion industry requires the latest runway styles.

It is incumbent upon job candidates and employees to find out what is expected of them and to dress accordingly. Job applicants can get the information they need by conducting online research for industry-specific attire, asking for advice from someone who works for an organization, or calling and inquiring about a company's dress code. One applicant did a "stakeout" by sitting in his car in a parking lot for a first-hand view of what employees were wearing. Employees will ensure they dress appropriately by adhering to the company's dress code or simply by observing how higher-ups in the organization dress.

In your research, you will come across a head-spinning array of categories of business dress. They will include business formal, business professional, traditional business, general business, and interview attire. You will also see business casual and its possible subdivisions of campus casual, active casual, sporty casual, smart casual, rugged casual, and small business casual. Then there is formal and semi-formal attire for special gala events. Knowing exactly what the categories mean is problematic because the interpretations vary so widely across organizations and industries. Do your best reconnaissance, and prepare for any error to be on the side of formality. Fortunately, the following business attire rules span industries.

BUSINESS ATTIRE RULES

- **Cleanliness.** Keep everything clean, including body, hair, clothing, nails, breath, and teeth. Keep a toothbrush and breath mints on hand for unexpected meetings.
- **Grooming.** Style hair in an acceptable fashion for your work environment. Avoid extreme colors and cuts unless that defines your company culture. Keep facial hair neat and trimmed. Wet hair is unprofessional, ear and nose hair are unsightly. With perfume, less is more.
- **Quality.** Fabric, stitching, pattern, color, buttonholes, and linings all give clues about the quality of a garment. Make sure they are top-notch.
- **Cost.** Employ the "cost per wearing method" before buying anything. A seemingly expensive item could cost just dollars per wearing.
- **Fit and condition.** Clothes need to fit well and be in good repair. Do not wear ripped, stained, frayed, or threadbare items or those that have missing buttons or holes.

- **Taste.** Avoid plunging necklines, garish colors, clanging bracelets, visible underwear, facial bolts, and conspicuous tattoos unless, of course, such styles define your workplace.

More than a few hiring managers have reported their dismay when the well-dressed millennials they hired bore no resemblance to those who came to work. It was as though they thought that once they landed the jobs, any additional sartorial efforts were unnecessary.

Older workers have their dress challenges, too. Some see no need to change styles that have served them well for 30, 40, or even 50 years. Others cling to the hope that the practical and conservative dress that comprises their wardrobes will once again be the standard. But attire, like everything, evolves with the times, and it's important to evolve with it.

The Right Way to Travel

"ON YOUR LEFT!" comes the loud shout. Today, for what must have been the hundredth time, Liz is practically run over on her walk to work by a passing bicyclist. Or at least it feels that way. Liz appreciates the positive impact more bicycles and fewer cars have on collective well-being and the environment. What she doesn't appreciate are the heart palpitations caused by a cyclist shouting in her ear as he speeds by with just inches to spare at 30 miles an hour. Startled, angry, and practically knocked off her feet—again—Liz begins to shout back at the cyclist, but he is long gone. "How can people be so inconsiderate?" Liz says out loud.

Liz's route to work is via Boston's Charles River, a beautiful and very popular location surrounded by trees and flat paved paths that go for more than 20 miles. In the course of a given day, thousands of runners, walkers, cyclists, bladers, moms with strollers, and dog lovers with their dogs all share the river's paths. But an unfortunate chasm has developed between cyclists and pedestrians, as each vociferously and indignantly laments the other faction's lack of consideration. And if she is honest with herself, Liz knows each side has valid complaints.

So Liz makes a decision. While she can't change everyone's attitude and behavior, she can change hers. When the next cyclist comes riding toward her, Liz gives her ample room to pass and smiles. To her amazement, the cyclist smiles back and thanks her. She tries this several more times and finds that almost everyone returns her smile, and some even say hello. Liz decides that showing a little courtesy toward those she encounters on her commute may just encourage others to do the same. No matter, it will make *her* commute more pleasant, and that's a start.

How do we annoy one another en route to work? Whether on foot or horseback (yes, a few folks do commute that way), in automobiles, or on buses, boats, mopeds, skateboards, planes, or trains, commuters are driven to daily distraction by their fellow travelers. Presuming that none of us set out to get others' blood boiling and are merely oblivious, the issue of traveling to and from work needs attention from a number of perspectives.

Employees begin to broadcast their brands the moment they leave home. Are they rushing down the sidewalk with ties undone and hair wet, bumping into slower moving pedestrians as they try to catch trains or buses? Do they push to get onto public transportation and vie for scarce open seats, giving scant, if any, thought to others? Are they impatient behind the wheel, weaving in and out of lanes, crudely gesturing at the slightest provocation and blaring horns with abandon? These behaviors do not go unnoticed.

Travel can be stressful, especially during rush hours. Meetings with clients, bosses, or coworkers, project deadlines, or relieving team members may all be dependent on our timeliness. Trying to deal with uncontrollable factors such as weather, traffic accidents, and breakdowns by giving vent to our frustrations may give us breakdowns of our own.

There are approximately 128.3 million commuters in the U.S., 76 percent of whom travel to and from work in their own cars. Another 12 percent carpool, and approximately 8 percent combined take the bus, walk, bicycle, or ride the subway. The rest use alternate means (horseback?). Where we live determines how we get to work. In cities, up to 15 percent of workers travel by foot and up to 5 percent by bicycle.[12]

To protect your brand and ensure safety all around, the following guidelines are offered for the various transportation modes.

WHEN IN AN AUTOMOBILE:

- **Personal auto:**

    Use good judgment and observe the rules of the road. Speeding, following too closely, flashing headlights, using the breakdown lane to bypass traffic, or zigzagging between lanes will win you no friends and may get you pulled over.

    DO NOT text or use social media while driving. The National Highway Transportation Safety Administration reports that in 2014, more than 3,000 people were killed in distracted driving-related car crashes, and 431,000 were injured. The average time eyes are off the road while texting is five seconds, which, if traveling at 55 MPH, is like covering the entire length of a football field blindfolded.[13]

Resist the urge to text even at stoplights. Invariably, the light will turn green, which you will know by the horns blaring behind you. You may make the light, but others will not, and this may come back to haunt you at the next intersection.

- **Carpool:**

  Establish costs and payment guidelines up front. If everyone takes turns driving, split all costs evenly. If one person does the driving, consider a mileage approach factoring in costs for fuel, maintenance, parking, and tolls. The IRS offers mileage rates, which it updates on a yearly basis.

  Keep on hand a list of co-riders' cell, work, home, and emergency phone numbers.

  Be ready when your ride arrives. Requiring others to wait is inconsiderate. Doing so habitually may get you kicked out of the carpool.

  Respect the culture of the carpool. If food and drink are allowed and conversation welcome, participate as you like. If instead, quiet is desired, observe that.

  Be meticulous about personal hygiene. Apply fragrance sparingly, if at all. Be neat, and take newspapers and trash with you.

Decide upon seating based upon practical considerations, such as the needs and the sizes of the passengers or drop-off order.

Stick like glue to the no-stopping policy. If anyone is ever to get to his destination, personal errands cannot be allowed.

Be reliable. If you are the driver and are sick or delayed, give your passengers as much notice as possible. Allow for unexpected traffic, construction, accidents, long lights, tollbooth backups, and weather delays.

- **Taxi and transportation services:**

Be respectful of the driver and of the automobile, and be aware that any bad behavior on your part may become part of a file on you. Uber and Lyft rate their customers and share this knowledge with fellow drivers who may elect not to pick you up in the future. (Want to know your rating? A feature on the Uber app lets you find out. Or just ask the driver!)

Engage the driver in conversation if you are so inclined, but only if he seems receptive to it. A driver's first priority is to get you safely to your destination, which may require his full attention to the road and directions.

Do not eat, drink, or engage in personal grooming while in the vehicle.

Keep calm if traffic or weather delays your ride, and, of course, do not blame the driver. He or she is equally, if not more, frustrated than you are.

WHEN ON A TRAIN OR BUS:

- Attend to personal grooming tasks before you board. This means no hair brushing, shaving (yes, it's done), nail filing or clipping, tooth picking, or applying makeup.
- Do not travel if you are sick. But if you decide you absolutely must, cover coughs and sneezes, and stand or sit as far away from others as possible.
- Allow passengers to get off a bus or train before you get on. Board quickly, being careful of others' toes, shins, elbows, and belongings. If you bump into someone, apologize.
- Do not eat or drink when commuting, especially on short commutes.
- Respect fellow travelers. Occupy no more room than that to which one person is entitled. Do not allow briefcases, luggage, or umbrellas to occupy needed sitting or standing room.
- Keep your voice down and music to yourself. Loud phone calls, conversations, and music distract and disturb fellow passengers who may be trying to work, rest, or think.

WHEN ON A PLANE:

- Comply with boarding instructions and then move to your seat as quickly as possible. Do not obstruct others as you stow your luggage. Move out of the aisle so others can pass.
- Remember, this is a public mode of transportation and other travelers' comfort, convenience, and safety are as important as yours. Take up the space, including storage and foot room, for which you paid and no more.
- Recline your seat, if you desire, but look back first and ask politely if you may do so. Yes, you are within your rights to

recline, but considering the person behind you who may be eating or working is just courteous. Do not ever employ a device that prevents others from reclining. Not only is that presumptuous, it is against airline rules. There are simple solutions to get more legroom: pay for it or fly with airlines that offer more space.

- Follow the instructions of the crew for seatbelt and electronic device use. Do not argue or cause a disruption. Airlines have zero tolerance for such behavior, and you may be required to deplane.
- Do not presume your seatmates want to engage in conversation. Read their nonverbal cues, and respect signals that they wish to work, read, or rest.
- Accept delays as part of travel. Everyone is in the same situation. Arguing with gate personnel makes you look like an inexperienced and unsophisticated traveler.

WHEN ON A BICYCLE:

- Obey all traffic signals and rules of the road.
- Make sure you and the bicycle are properly equipped.
- Use hand signals to alert others of your intentions.
- Give notice before passing and a wide berth when doing so. Try not to startle pedestrians or other riders as you pass by them.

WHEN ON FOOT:

- Watch where you're going. Observe traffic signals and never try to beat a light, especially when there is oncoming traffic. Do not assume drivers see you.

- Step aside to use your electronic device. Texting and taking photos, especially with selfie sticks, are to be avoided in the middle of a sidewalk. They can slow you down, cause you to abruptly stop or collide with someone or something, or even cause you to walk into traffic. Using earbuds that restrict hearing is equally dangerous.
- Keep to the right on the sidewalk, and try to keep a brisk pace so others do not continually need to pass you. Be considerate of those who are slower, the elderly, persons with disabilities, and those pushing strollers or with arms full of groceries.
- Do not walk two-, three-, or even four-abreast or have impromptu mid-sidewalk meetings. Others may be forced into traffic to get around you.

Getting the ingredients right to achieve the highest level of professional presence enables employees to present their best versions of themselves in the workplace.

REMEMBER

- Develop and display an all-star personal brand.
- Embrace a stellar attitude.
- Attire yourself appropriately for your corporate culture.
- Realize that small behaviors make big impressions.

chapter 4

business behavior

Combining Proven Strategies with 21st Century Expectations

"It takes 20 years to build a reputation and five minutes to ruin it."

—WARREN BUFFETT

Kate has spent months cultivating a business relationship with a very successful, soon-to-be retiring executive. She has outlined the ambitious plan she proposes for his retirement account, suggesting the prospect of very healthy growth and a comfortable yearly income. Kate, a 38-year-old wealth management advisor, knows that for Robert, a conservative gentleman, it is important that he work with a firm that shares his values. Kate also knows there is a lot of competition for his business. But they seem to have developed a nice, respectful rapport, and she thinks he may be ready to commit. Kate's fingers are crossed. This next call could close the deal.

The call goes well, and as it winds down Kate asks Robert when they can meet to share more information and sign formal papers. At that very moment, her colleague in the next cubicle, who is arguing on the phone with his ex-wife, shouts out a stream of obscenities that can be heard throughout the entire office. Kate freezes. Her client goes silent. Then he clears his throat and says, "Thank you, I think I have all the information I need. I will let you know if I plan to move forward. Good-bye."

Here you are with your newly burnished brand, your finely adjusted attitude, and your perfectly appropriate attire. You've even managed to travel to work with life and limb intact. You are someone about to start a new job and will allow nothing to derail what promises to be your banner first day! There's just one more thing to consider. The culture of the organization you have just joined is one that can only be fully appreciated from the *inside*. You've done your due diligence and know as much as any outsider could possibly know about this organization. So it's a bit of a shock to discover how different things are on the other side of the glass door.

The Glass Door

Jake, 23 years old and eight months on the job, only wishes he had known when he started what he knows now. His job as a representative at a call center had been described as simple and pressure-free: He would answer callers' questions about products, and if they expressed interest in buying, he would transfer them to the sales department to handle the sales. The first couple of months were fun as Jake learned about the products and bonded with the other new hires. But once he was on the phone full-time, this "no-pressure" job turned into anything but.

Jake was quickly informed that too many of the calls he was sending through to the sales department were unqualified prospects, wasting the sales representatives' time. He also learned that the number and length of his calls were measured, his conversations were monitored, his emails were counted, and his time on social media was logged. And all of these statistics would factor into his job evaluation, affecting any potential pay raise or promotion.

During the interview process, Jake had been delighted to hear about the company's unlimited vacation policy, flexible schedules, and flat organizational structure that gave employees unfettered access to the higher-ups. "How great was that nap room!" he said to himself at the time. But Jake soon realized that no one actually used any of these highly touted benefits, as though there was some unwritten rule against it. And although they had access to the executives' calendars to schedule meetings with them, no one ever did. Instead, there was not-so-subtle pressure to stay late, forgo vacation time, and keep one's ideas and concerns to oneself. Jake knew he was in the real world now. He just hadn't anticipated what reality would look like or how fast it would be upon him.

A surprise awaiting digital natives in particular is that the flat organizational structure they envisioned is not so flat after all. Designed to eliminate unnecessary layers of management and foster collaboration, decision-making, and creativity, the flat structure is particularly attractive to millennials eager to share their ideas. It's not just young start-up companies with little hierarchical structure to dismantle or e-commerce companies like Zappos that have embraced flatness. Staid manufacturing companies like General Motors are also dipping their toes in the flat waters. According to Tim Kastelle in

Harvard Business Review, "There is a growing body of evidence that shows organizations with flat structures outperform those with more traditional hierarchies in most situations."[1]

If there is agreement that flatter is better in theory, there is less agreement on whether it works in practice and whether organizations are actually as flat as they claim to be. Google itself dabbled in this approach back in 2002 when it decided to do away with the management level in its engineering operations, but within months, management was back. Going forward, there will likely be degrees of flatness determined on a company-by-company basis. To be on the safe side, new employees will want to find out what kind of structures their organizations have and make no assumptions.

Penni Connor, a vice president at the Fortune 500 energy company Eversource, says, "Eversource is deliberately trying to create a workplace that encourages entrepreneurial thinking." She also says there is a time and place for sharing. "In a rush to get their questions answered, there is no hesitancy (among millennials) to take their questions right to a higher-up who could answer it, but is not necessarily the best person to answer it." She adds, "They need to ask themselves how to navigate the hierarchy better."

Older workers used to a hierarchical structure can also make missteps. If their new culture is one that not only encourages but also expects employees to speak up, holding back will do them no service. Become keenly attuned to expectations within your organization, and proceed with caution. Your CEO may welcome weekend texts from employees, and if so, text away. But you'll want to make sure of that *before* you interrupt his golf game, a dinner party, or a nap.

What awaits you on your first day is a plethora of people, all eager to pass and share judgment about you, the new kid. You're a curiosity to all, a threat to some, and more work for others. Your attitude, energy level, attire, style, demeanor, confidence, judgment, grace, and overall professionalism will say volumes about you, even before you've had a chance to say "good morning." Your level of comfort and skill in making polite conversation will add to what becomes a practically indelible first impression—the only first impression you'll get to make. The success of your first day may have an unalterable impact on the success of all of your future days. It is wise to execute it thoughtfully.

THE FIRST DAY

- **Arrive early.** Be well rested, well dressed, and raring to go. Shake hands and introduce yourself to colleagues, and try to remember their names.
- **Thank everyone.** Thank the person who announces your arrival, escorts you to your desk, arranges for your security badge, sets up your technology, walks you through stacks of paperwork, directs you to the break room and restroom, invites you to lunch, and offers you information. Your gratitude will be remembered.
- **Look and listen.** Pay attention to the general office vibe. When do people arrive? How quickly do they get to work? How do they interact with one another? When do they leave? What is the noise level? Respect the culture and follow suit.
- **Take notes.** Record important information on your phone or a notepad. Having new codes, names, numbers, and emails at your fingertips will help you assimilate quickly.

Everyday Manners

Brimming with confidence, Connie had aced her telephone and Skype interviews for a fabulous new job as a sales manager with a leading consumer products company. She has one more hurdle today, the in-person interview, after which Connie believes the job will be hers!

An experienced 34-year-old sales professional, Connie is confident but is taking no chances. She leaves three hours early for a drive that would usually take two hours, getting to the company parking lot with plenty of time to spare. Connie had decided she would do her hair and makeup when she arrived, to look as fresh as possible.

She drives around to the quiet far side of the building, out of sight of parked cars or incoming traffic, and picks a sunny spot for good light. She brought her portable curling iron and begins curling and spraying her hair. Perfect, she thinks! In the bright light, she notices and tweezes a few stray hairs on her eyebrows. She adjusts her bra straps and her blouse and after a quick underarm "sniff test," applies a little more antiperspirant. "Just to be safe," she thinks. She brushes and flosses her teeth, looking in the car mirror to make sure there are no leftover poppy seeds from this morning's breakfast bagel. She swishes around some mouthwash then spits it into her cold coffee. She puts on her lipstick, rubbing with her little finger a bit that had gotten onto her tooth. Finally, she pours the mouthwash and remaining coffee on the ground. Finished.

With a satisfied smile, Connie drives to the building's entrance, parks, and enters. It takes a while for the hiring manager to arrive and escort her to his office. He seems to avoid making eye contact with her. Is he shy? As they make their way down the long corridor, Connie struggles to make small talk, to no avail, and begins to experience a growing sense of dread.

As the door to his office opens, Connie sees the view immediately outside his window. It is exactly where she was parked just minutes ago, performing her beauty and personal grooming rituals in the brightest, whitest sunlight.

Each day, people who have a great deal of influence over our current and future careers have their eyes peeled and their antennae up. The good news is we have a great deal of control over how others perceive us. It's just a matter of making the right decisions.

PAY ATTENTION TO OTHERS

- Do you look back as you walk into a building to see who might be coming in behind you, or do you absentmindedly let doors shut on coworkers?
- Do you cheerfully greet security personnel by name or treat them as if they were invisible?
- Do you look up when walking in corridors, or are you glued to your device, oblivious to the passersby?
- Do you check to see who might also be trying to catch the elevator, or do you hit "close" the minute you are aboard?
- Do you keep right on stairs or position yourself squarely in the middle, impeding others trying to get by?
- Do you talk loudly on the way to your desk or keep the decibel level down out of respect for colleagues who are working?

The number of ways in which colleagues can potentially offend or irritate others before buckling down to work each day pales only in comparison to the opportunities they have to do so once the workday begins. These unintentional behaviors may seem trivial, but when regularly subjected to them, they become a monumental nuisance. Resentment builds, relationships suffer, and brands are bruised, all for want of a little common courtesy.

What annoys people at work? The list is *very, very* long. It includes not allowing others to get off of elevators before getting on, constant tardiness, leaving dirty cups and dishes in the lunchroom, wafting food aromas, personal grooming at desks (nail-clipping, flossing, hair-brushing, etc.), poor personal hygiene, incessant and loud personal calls, gum-chewing, loud talking, humming, whistling, singing, noise-emitting electronic devices, conducting conference calls and speakerphone conversations in open spaces, never contributing to collections for gifts, coming back late from breaks, not reimbursing coworkers for miscellaneous expenses, never making coffee or lunch runs, always asking for but never having stamps (or tissues, gum, mints, etc.), eavesdropping, noisy jewelry, heavy walking, foot-tapping, finger-drumming, knuckle-cracking, throat-clearing, nose-blowing, pen-clicking, and sniffling.

The list goes on.

Staring, failing to observe personal space boundaries, lurking outside someone's cubicle or office door, interrupting others' work instead of calling or emailing ahead, reading coworkers' computer screens, emptying but never refilling candy jars, incessantly talking about new babies (or relationships, homes, cars, etc.), being overly dramatic, being lazy, boasting, yelling, arguing, swearing, fist-banging, door-slamming, leaving break rooms (or restrooms or meeting rooms) dirty, taking up too much parking lot space, stealing food, leaving coffee pots (or water jugs or copy paper trays) empty, slurping coffee, eating noisily, pranking, dressing inappropriately, not thanking others for holding doors, laughing or commenting out loud at text messages or emails, not asking permission before borrowing others' property, not returning borrowed items, emitting bodily sounds and odors, decorating office spaces unprofessionally, and currying favor with bosses.

The advice regarding these behaviors is simple: *don't.* As Henry Ford, Sr., said, "Paying attention to the little things that most men neglect makes a few men rich."

Business Meetings

Did you ever wonder just how much time people spend in meetings? According to a study by the Australian software company Atlassian, most employees attend 62 meetings a month of which 50 percent are considered time wasted. During an average 31 hours per month in meetings, 91 percent of employees daydream, 73 percent do other work, 47 percent complain, and 39 percent sleep. The cost of unnecessary meetings in the U.S. per year: an eye-popping $37 billion in salary.[2]

Regardless, executives overwhelmingly agree that face-to-face meetings are still the best way to persuade, lead, engage, and make decisions. Rather than do away with meetings entirely, simple strategies can be employed to make yours as productive as possible.

MAKE SURE YOU ARE NOT THE ORGANIZER WHO:

- Fails to have a valid reason for the meeting, invite the right people, or send an agenda
- Neglects to reserve a meeting room, test AV, or order materials and refreshments
- Forgets to send pre-meeting assignments or reading or to advise attendees what will be expected of them
- Schedules ill-timed meetings such as early Monday morning or late Friday afternoon
- Fails to intervene when attendees show disrespect through words or behaviors

The biggest complaint about meetings by far is that they were not necessary to begin with. These complaints are valid if the information could have been communicated in other, better ways, if key stakeholders were not available, if there was not enough time to prepare, or if nothing would have been gained in holding the meetings.

FLAWLESS MEETINGS

- **Invite only those who can contribute to and/or benefit from attending.** These include both stakeholders and opponents. Send agendas and assignments/reading in advance. You need not invite higher-ups, but inform them of meetings and let them know they are welcome to attend.
- **Prepare tent cards.** This is especially important when attendees do not know one another, and it's a nice touch even when they do. At formal meetings, decide on seating and arrange tent cards accordingly. Make introductions,

invite attendees to help themselves to refreshments, and let them know where the restrooms are located.

- **Consider timing of meetings.** Early mornings when people are fresh are great if high participation is required. Mid- and late-morning meetings are good as long as they do not run into lunch. Lunch meetings can work well, as long as attendees are fed! Mid-afternoon meetings require energetic presenters, activities, or engaging topics to keep people awake. Late afternoon meetings are fine if they do not conflict with departures.
- **Set meeting expectations up front.** These include how and when attendees will be asked to contribute, when breaks can be expected, and whether using devices is permitted. Electronic device use at meetings can be a big problem because others often feel disrespected or ignored. A client told me that the person using a device is saying, "You are not worthy of my time." The culture of the group may allow it, but unless everyone is on his or her device, it is wise to stay off of yours.
- **Thank people for their attendance.** Discuss next steps, and then confirm them in an email.

Adhering to these guidelines will stand you in good stead. If, in addition to these, you start on time, stick to the agenda, and end on time, you will be inducted into the meeting organizer hall of fame!

Attending a Meeting

As a meeting attendee, you also have responsibilities. What you do before, during, and after a meeting will be critical to its success.

Occasionally, you will be invited to a meeting and wonder why. It may have been a courtesy invitation or, possibly, an invitation sent by mistake. If you are ever unsure about why you were invited, it is perfectly permissible to ask the organizer. In some cases, you will have the opportunity to gracefully bow out.

- **Arrive early and prepared.** Introduce yourself to other attendees and take advantage of this golden opportunity to "work the room." Be sure to comply with instructions given by the meeting chair about seating, breaks, participation, and electronic device use.
- **Respect others' opinions.** Do not interrupt, argue, or hold side conversations.
- **Display attentive body language.** Do not slouch, cross your arms, roll your eyes, look out the window, frown, shake your head, yawn, doze off, or doodle.
- **Stay in your seat.** If you think there is a chance an emergency might arise, such as a call about a sick child or expectant wife, ask the meeting chair beforehand if it would be all right for you to keep your phone on for this reason only. But even then, keep it out of view and silent.
- **Take notes on a laptop or tablet if allowed.** But do not get caught doing anything extracurricular.

The Team

Today's workplace is all about teams, and it's easy to see why. Put together a group of people with diverse backgrounds, experiences, perspectives, and talents, and a more creative solution to a problem or situation is sure to follow. The benefits that accrue to organizations and employees from effective team interactions include greater productivity, better human resource utilization, increased learning, improved morale, and greater efficiency. The bottom line is that when people work together in a positive fashion toward a common goal, anything is possible.

But it's not always easy. Egos get in the way. And if they do, conflicts arise, resentments build, power struggles develop, alliances form, and feelings get hurt. The result is wasted time, energy, and resources. If teams *do* work effectively, it is because members have taken personal responsibility to do their respective parts.

TEAM MEMBERS

- **Polish their attitudes.** The nature of a team is to bring together divergent views and experiences to achieve the best possible result. Disagreements are welcomed but disagreeable behaviors are not. Effective team members show respect, humility, a willingness to learn, and an acceptance of the wisdom of the collective. They keep calm even when others do not and keep the focus on the issue at hand.

- **Hone listening skills.** Good team members encourage others to share their expertise through active, attentive, and respectful listening. They never argue or interrupt, but instead allow others to express themselves as they choose, presuming it is respectful of other attendees.

- **Exhibit exemplary verbal and nonverbal communication skills.** Good team members are respectful in their tones, words, and body language. They always take the high road.

- **Execute their responsibilities.** Good team members are responsible, responsive, thorough, and timely. They never pass the buck or lose sight of the team's goal.

The Cubicle Farm

Patrice cringes. Here comes Dottie, and she looks like she wants to talk. Again. Patrice likes Dottie, but she comes into Patrice's cubicle three or four times a day to talk about whatever is on her mind. The topic could be anything—her brilliant new grandson's most recent milestones, the latest company gossip, a recap of last night's TV shows, or the weekend weather forecast—no thought goes unshared.

The problem is, every visit breaks Patrice's concentration. She has tried every subtle means she can think of to discourage Dottie, from keeping her eyes on her computer screen when she approaches to piling her office chair with books and binders so there is no place for her to sit. Sometimes she offers Dottie only a brief smile or a one-word acknowledgment to her greetings, and she has even said, "Sorry, I was concentrating. What did you say?" But none of these have worked.

So Patrice decides it's time to be direct. She gently tells Dottie that to keep on task, she needs to keep their visits to break times. Not the least bit offended, Dottie says, "I only stopped by because I thought you really liked my visits. You should have just told me. Really!" Problem solved.

Today's workplace looks nothing like what digital immigrants remember when they joined the workforce pre-1990. Then, it was primarily comprised of offices, with sizes and locations determined by hierarchy and rank. Executives occupied large, beautifully appointed, carpeted corner offices with magnificent top-floor views. Everyone else worked on floors below in spaces and square feet determined by their positions and tasks. There was little collaboration between the ranks. If a worker was unlucky enough to be "called on the carpet" for a conversation with an executive, it was *not* a good thing. Open-plan spaces did exist, but were reserved for entry-level employees or those who performed specific functions such as clerical staff.

The office has changed dramatically, largely because of technology. Employees now also work from their homes, cars, hotel rooms, or local coffee shops. Business is conducted on a treadmill, a train, or a plane. Today, 9 to 5 is 24-7. The corner office, if it exists, has walls made of glass. But offices are hard to come by because collaboration is king, and the open-plan layout is its castle.

The Open Office

Creativity. Productivity. Agility. These are the promises of the new workplace. Designed to encourage communication and improve effectiveness, in open-plan offices, employee work side by side at desks, in chairs, or at long tables. They stand, they sit, they wander. According to the International Management Facility Association, a full 70 percent of U.S. employees currently work in such an environment.[3]

In concept, the design makes sense. But in reality, it has its challenges. Studies show that the majority of employees are not happy about open-plan offices, citing lack of privacy as their greatest concern. A study by the global design firm Gensler reveals that open-plan offices actually lower productivity and focus and significantly increase sick days.[4] Tenured workers in particular may have a hard time adjusting to the concept, especially if it means giving up the cherished privacy and status they equate with private offices. But technology giants such as Google, Facebook, and Twitter are all on board, and such traditionally conservative industries as insurance and financial services are increasingly adopting the concept. Love it or loathe it, open-plan is the new standard.

The form and function of the entire office is evolving. Companies are going to great lengths to design spaces in which ideas can be captured from chance encounters. Among them are wider staircases that allow for side-by-side conversation, booths in lobbies and lunchrooms for spontaneous brainstorming, bar-stools in cafes for tête-à-tête communication, free transportation shuttles for sharing ideas with seatmates, and on-site laundry facilities for impromptu discourse over the dry cycle.

Employees may not agree on the merits of today's workplace evolution, but they can perhaps mutually agree on best behaviors for working within them.

Cubicle Life

If you still happen to work in a cubicle, you will notice its size is shrinking and its walls are lower. Cubicle dwellers face challenges in getting work done without interrupting, or being interrupted by, neighbors just inches away.

POLITE POINTS

- **Keep volume low.** This applies to conversations, music, and electronic devices. Use earphones, mute devices, and conduct speakerphone conversations and meetings in spaces designed for these purposes.

- **Don't eat at your desk.** Pungent foods, such as Indian or Mexican food, or reheated fish, are not welcomed aromas for many. If you do eat at your desk, dispose of food wrappers in appropriate receptacles.

- **Be aware of all olfactory issues.** Fragrance, worn gym clothing, and bare feet can be unpleasant smelling to those nearby.

- **Keep décor tasteful.** Tasteful photos, appropriate objet d'art, quality desk accessories, and small plants are fine. Do not display items that could be considered offensive or controversial. If you wouldn't say it, don't display it!

- **Respect coworkers' privacy.** Do not enter cubicles unless invited, read others' computer screens, touch others' belongings, help yourself to coworkers' candy or snacks, purposely listen in on conversations, or comment on anything overheard.

Common Areas

Using common amenities and areas requires a great deal of trust and honesty among coworkers. Incredibly, employee theft in general and theft of coworkers' food in particular are extremely common occurrences. According to a 2015 report by statisticbrain.com, employee theft amounts to *$50 billion* per year, and 75 percent of employees admit to having stolen at work at least once.[5] *Inc.* magazine says 43 percent of employees report they have had food stolen from them.[6] A good rule of thumb to employ: Unless you brought it, bought it, or someone expressly invited you to it, do not help yourself to anything. This also applies to food left in common areas after lunches and meetings. While it may seem to be there for the taking, there could be plans for the food, and you may be advised of this while helping yourself to it.

If you decide to take advantage of any of the common areas available to you for collaboration or privacy, resist any temptation to take up residence in them. We all want and need privacy from time to time, but common areas are meant to serve as temporary oases, not permanent solutions to privacy quests.

The New Schedules

"This is not working," a frustrated Grace says under her breath. A 43-year-old career advisor at Jefferson Junior College, Grace recently returned to her job after a five-year hiatus following the birth of her daughter. She was happy when a new job-sharing arrangement with her colleague, Jim, a long-time employee, presented itself. Jim had been on the verge of retiring but decided a part-time paycheck would be perfect as he got his gardening business off the ground. Grace thought it would work well for her, too, because she would be able to drop off and pick up her young daughter from school three days a week.

It's only been a few weeks, but the arrangement is beginning to fray. Increasingly, Grace feels like she is doing much more than her share and that Jim's communication is woefully lacking. Just yesterday, a recruiting visit they were supposed to arrange for a key local employer fell through because Jim did not let Grace know that the recruiter was expecting to hear from her. It's like Jim's mind is elsewhere, probably on his new gardening business, Grace thinks.

Grace cannot do this entire job by herself. She has spoken with Jim, who promised to do better. But nothing has improved. Grace hates the thought of going to their boss, but cannot think of another alternative.

Telecommuting, flextime, part-time, and job-sharing have changed how often and during what hours employees come to the office, and even if they come at all. Driven by millennials, this flexible approach to work is what this cohort wants and expects. Older workers like it, too. Depending upon what you do, it is likely your organization does or soon will offer some kind of flexible work arrangement.

Telecommuting

The popularity of telecommuting among employees and employers alike has gained huge traction. Advocates of tele-commuting, generally defined as an employment arrangement where employees work at least half of the time at home, point to increased productivity, improved job satisfaction, and saved time and money. Employers benefit by reduced employee attrition as well as substantial savings on costs associated with providing office space.

Telecommuting is not for everyone. Some employers simply do not trust workers to be self-directed and motivated enough to get their work done at home. Some managers feel threatened by the arrangement, wondering if their positions are redundant. And some employees who have tried it reported experiencing loneliness and difficulty in setting clear boundaries between their professional and personal lives.

To achieve the best results, telecommuters should organize their workdays with the same dedication and professionalism they would if their bosses were sitting right next to them. Yes, a home-office worker does have the opportunity to throw in the occasional load of laundry during the day, but generally looks at this workday as he would any other: as the opportunity to produce an excellent work effort in exchange for a paycheck.

MAKING TELECOMMUTING WORK

- **Create an office space.** Start at a designated time, take regularly scheduled breaks, and at the end of the day, close the office door. A business associate of mine says to get herself in the right frame of mind each day, she dresses professionally, leaves the house to get coffee, and returns promptly at 8:00 A.M. to start her day. Make sure friends know your working hours and that, unless it is important, you are not to be disturbed.

- **Dress the part every day.** Even if you don't see anyone face-to-face, attire still matters. A study from the Kellogg School of Management found that the symbolic meaning clothing holds for people might affect their productivity.[7] Besides, you never know when you might get called to a Skype meeting.

- **Communicate, communicate, and communicate!** You need never be out of the loop if you keep yourself firmly in it. Use technology to stay on top of others' minds. And do not forget the telephone. The sound of a human voice has its own immeasurable magic.

- **Arrange face-to-face meetings with your team and boss.** Attend company events and after-hours celebrations. It lets others know you are still very much involved.

On-site part-time and flextime employees will incorporate similar strategies around their schedules, particularly if they do not overlap with their bosses' and colleagues' schedules. Punctuality and reliability are key for part-time and flextime workers.

Sharing an Office

When telecommuters eventually come to the office, they need somewhere to sit! Enter "hoteling" and "hot-desking." The terms are often used interchangeably, but there is a distinction between the two. Hoteling is reservation-based unassigned office seating, while hot-desking is reservationless unassigned seating. Both are designed to provide dedicated, supported office space for those who only need it occasionally. In addition to adhering to the guidelines for open-plan spaces, a considerate hoteler or hot-desker observes these rules.

GUIDELINES

- **Reserve only needed time and space.** Cancel reservations you no longer need or can't use. Tying up space unnecessarily may impact your ability to secure future reservations.
- **Introduce yourself.** Smile and offer a friendly greeting to those sitting nearby, but take care not to interrupt them if they are obviously busy or concentrating on work.
- **Keep the space clean.** Sanitize all surfaces and equipment with disinfectant wipes upon arriving and departing. Take trash with you when you vacate.
- **Leave the space as you found it.** Store personal items in desk drawers while using the space, and make sure to take

them with you when you leave. Do not rearrange or remove furnishings.

Sharing a Job

The concept of job-sharing is increasingly the answer for parents wanting more time with their children, millennials interested in volunteering, older workers looking to design their "portfolio lives," and employees seeking less stress and more work-life integration. Employers benefit, too, from improved employee engagement and retention, increased accountability and productivity, and the combined intelligence, experience, and perspective of two employees.

Employers can help ensure the success of job-sharing by pairing employees with complementary skills and temperaments, setting clear expectations, and supporting efforts through ongoing feedback and coaching. Job-sharing partners will explicitly define their roles, agree upon reporting methods and frequency, communicate consistently, hold themselves and one another accountable, learn to respectfully disagree and reach consensus, present a unified front, and share both the responsibility for, and success of, their efforts.

The Benefits Buffet

Forty-one year-old Lori was a billing department representative at a large hospital. For 12 years, she had juggled the responsibilities of two children and a Monday through Friday 9 to 5 job, an hour away from home. After work, she'd go grocery shopping and hurry home to make dinner, hoping to spend at least a little time with her young daughters before it was time for bed.

It bothered Lori tremendously that her job made it impossible for her to attend any of her girls' school plays or soccer games, even though they never complained. (Well, maybe they complained a little.) But the billing department needed staffing during normal work hours, and Lori needed her job. And so when it was announced that the billing office hours were being expanded to 7:00 A.M. to 7:00 P.M. and that employees could now self-schedule their hours, Lori was elated. Lori did not know who was more excited—her nine-year-old daughter or herself! Today, for the first time that did not involve her taking personal or vacation time, Lori was going to see her little girl play soccer. The cookies made, Lori would be there on the sidelines, cheering away and smiling from ear to ear.

Are you a parent concerned about new baby expenses? Facebook has you covered with $4,000 in "Baby Cash." Worried about how to feed that new baby while traveling for work? Zillow will pay for moms to ship their breastmilk home. Travel bug biting? Airbnb will give you a $2,000 travel stipend to any of its lodgings worldwide. Eager to finally finish (or start) your novel? Deloitte will pay you for four weeks off, for any reason at all, and another three to six months at partial pay for volunteer work or a career-enhancing opportunity.

Employers know perks matter. According to a Glassdoor survey, "nearly three in five (57 percent) people report benefits and perks being among their top considerations before accepting a job, while four in five people say they would prefer new perks over a pay raise."[8] The same report indicates that while perks may get key talent in the door, they will not necessarily keep them there. Once on board, a company's culture, values, senior leadership, and career opportunities are the things that get the best to stay.

Subsidized transportation, company paid meals, dry cleaning services, and closing early on Fridays in the summer are now almost ubiquitous. Depending on the industry and company, today's work-life smorgasbord might include concierge services, web-monitored day care, adoption subsidies, family leave, prayer rooms, tax preparation assistance, paid volunteer time, free subscriptions, pet sitting, massages, on-site doctor's visits, nap pods, organic food, wine bars, home cleaning services, marital counseling, vacation money, help for aging parents and grandparents, in-home dinner delivery, international assignments, and paid sabbaticals.

Perks are defining the workplace. In the *New York Times* article "Housecleaning, Then Dinner? Silicon Perks Come Home," Matt Ritchel says, "That shifting mind-set—the idea that life and work must be blended rather than separated—is increasingly common." The article quotes Google spokesman Jordan Newman saying, "What you've seen is benefits moving away from free food into thinking more holistically about individuals and their health."[9]

Amenities cannot make up for bad corporate cultures and, if they are seen as ways to buy employees off, can even backfire. But if the culture is healthy, and everyone is happy, perks can provide a win-win situation.

The New Realities

The 21st century workplace can be disconcerting, even as employers try to make the lives of their employees ever more comfortable. Recognition of new workplace realities is everyone's responsibility. This starts with accepting the fact that we are under digital and visual surveillance many of our waking moments and virtually all of our working moments. Our commutes are chronicled by tollbooths, stoplights, and highway cameras that take our pictures while recording tolls paid, lights run, and speeds travelled. Mobile phones track our movements. Office parking lots, garages, entrances, and elevators are watched. Walks through security and to desks are logged. And once at our desks, Internet use, email communication, and telephone calls are monitored.

In the *Financial Times*, Adam Jones writes, "The Spies in the cellar are now sidling up to your desk." He says, "Offices, in particular, are becoming havens for monitoring equipment with varying levels of intrusiveness."[10] Among them, he writes, are sensors in name badges that monitor how people move around the office, who they talk to, and even their tone of voice. Workplace occupancy sensors indicate how often desks and meeting places are used.

Organizations defend these and other measures as ways to identify problem workers, maximize resources, and save costs. While few would object to the green benefits of smart rooms turning off lights when unoccupied, we find it disconcerting to realize that these rooms also know exactly when and for how long we are in them. Those seemingly unnoticed late arrivals, long lunches, and early weekend departures are perhaps not so unnoticed after all.

Perhaps this is not a problem in laid-back cultures, but it could be in more formal ones. Debating whether such monitoring is legal (it is), whether the information it provides to employers is useful (it is), whether the atmosphere it promotes feels like

"Big Brother is watching you" (it does), and whether employees like it (they do not) are all nonstarters. As with all elements of corporate culture, our options are these: Accept them, reject them and join new ones, or start our own. The surveilled workplace will become more and more the norm.

Success in today's professional arena requires more than a job well done. Surviving and thriving requires that you accept the realities of the new workplace and manage them as well as possible.

REMEMBER

- **Everything is different on the other side of "the glass door."** Your agility in adjusting to a new corporate culture will determine your chances for success and happiness within it.
- **Know that everyday manners matter more than anything else.** Good manners define your character and brand. Pay careful attention to the little things. They are huge.
- **Evolve with and embrace new workspaces.** Or start your own.
- **Respect your colleagues' work arrangements, hours, and time zones.** Consider these before scheduling meetings or otherwise attempting to engage with them.
- **Know that workplace realities mean that our brands are *always* on display. Always!**

chapter 5

business communication

Making the Connection

"Speak clearly, if you speak at all; carve every word before you let it fall."

—OLIVER WENDELL HOLMES, SR.

Today is the day. After a long process of winnowing candidates for an associate's position at a leading real estate law firm, Rebecca has narrowed it down to two: Paul and Frederick. On paper, there is no comparison. Frederick was on the law review at one of the country's top-tier law schools, graduating at the head of his class. The latest in a long line of very successful lawyers in his family, his social connections and avid interest in golf and sailing make him a natural to rub elbows with just the kind of clients the firm is looking to attract. Frederick dresses impeccably from head to toe. And he is confident—maybe too confident—Rebecca thinks, as she remembered how he jumped in to finish her sentences and dropped names with abandon.

Paul had also graduated first in his class, but from a second-tier school. His LSATs would have gotten him into a top school, but he needed to attend part-time so he could work to support himself and his young family. This let the elite schools out. Paul did not have Frederick's social connections, expensive hobbies, or bespoke wardrobe. What he did have, Rebecca thought, was a respectful nature, a quiet self-assuredness, and a genuine warmth. When Rebecca spoke, Paul listened intently. He asked excellent questions, deftly responded to her comments, added relevant information, and smiled and laughed when appropriate. He made Rebecca feel like his primary interest was how he could help the firm, *not* how lucky the firm would be to hire him. Considering the many obstacles Paul had overcome to get to the finalist stage and the kind, respectful way in which he communicated with her, Rebecca was sure his intelligence, tenacity, and authenticity would serve the firm and its clients very well. Her decision was made.

Well-honed communication skills are necessary at every stage of one's career, but are even more critical as one ascends—or tries to ascend—the corporate ladder. One need look no further than to Doug McMillan to support this point. At 49 years old, he is the youngest Walmart CEO since Sam Walton and is by all accounts a brilliant communicator. Named to Decker Communications' "The Top Ten Best (and Worst) Communicators of 2015,"[1] he is described as a warm, humble, approachable man who communicates care for his employees. Walmart board member Kevin Systrom, cofounder and CEO of Instagram, agrees. In *Fortune*'s 2015 article entitled "The Man Who's Reinventing Walmart,"[2] Brian O'Keefe describes Mr. McMillan as the most intensely friendly person he has ever met. He says that "his focus is on you, like there is no other thing going on in his mind when he talks to you. He's not distracted, he's 100 percent focused on you."

Walmart's CEO seems to have taken the advice of its founder to heart. So important was good communication to Sam Walton that he devoted 2 of his "10 Rules for Building a Business"[3] to it. Mr. Walton advised:

> **Rule 4.** *Communicate everything you can to your partners. The more they know, the more they'll understand. The more they understand, the more they'll care. Once they care, there is no stopping them.*
>
> **Rule 7.** *Listen to everyone in your company. And figure out ways to get them talking. To push responsibility down within your organization, and to force good ideas to bubble up within it, you must listen to what your associates are trying to tell you.*

Communication can make or break business relationships, careers, and even companies. Effective communication provides you with opportunities to expand networks, raise profiles, showcase skills, and engender confidence. Despite all these benefits, developing good communication skills is still an intimidating prospect for many.

Conversation, especially spontaneous, unscripted small talk, is particularly problematic. Millennials would rather do anything than engage in simple conversation, finding it superficial, boring, pointless, and altogether too much work. Chatting, unless it's via electronic devices, is just not their thing. Truth be told, older generations are not too crazy about small talk either. But it's very important, because substantive conversations, crucial to professional success, emerge from small talk.

Opportunities for conversation are everywhere, and the professionally savvy take advantage of as many as possible as often as possible. The chances to promote one's personal brand through conversation are endless: on public transportation, while waiting in line for coffee, walking down a hallway, or riding an elevator, and at business meetings, lunches, dinners, events, parties, or conferences.

Nonverbal Cues

Liam needs advice from his boss. The 33-year-old biotech engineer is not sure how to proceed with the new project he's been assigned. He approaches his boss's office and peering through the window, sees him hunched over his computer screen in deep concentration, frowning intently. The thought quickly flits through Liam's mind that his boss is probably working on the quarterly reports due later today. He quickly brushes that thought aside and says to himself, "This will just take a second."

When Liam tentatively knocks, his boss looks up with an impatient "this had better be important" expression on his face—an expression lost on Liam. He clears his throat and asks his question. His boss, incredulous as well as annoyed, shakes his head and says, "You interrupted me for that?"

The ability to read and send nonverbal cues is critical in the professional arena. In face-to-face interactions, studies tell us that approximately 60 percent of communication is nonverbal,

30 percent is tone of voice, and only 10 percent is the words we say. Nonverbal communication governs how we think about ourselves, according to Amy Cuddy, social psychologist and associate professor at Harvard Business School. In her TED talk, "Your Body Language Shapes Who You Are," she says, "Our bodies change our minds, our minds change our behaviors, our behaviors change our outcomes."[4]

Ms. Cuddy says to convey high power—and conceivably change our minds in the process—we should lean in, stand with our heads high, our arms open, our legs uncrossed, and our hands on our hips or clasped behind our necks. Conversely, we would avoid the appearance of low power by refraining from looking down, having our hands in our pockets, crossing our arms and legs, or slouching. Ms. Cuddy recommends that we not only "fake it 'til we make it" with our nonverbal communication, but fake it until we actually become as strong and confident as our body language conveys. There is not complete agreement that nonverbal communication changes minds, but there is virtually universal agreement that nonverbal communication affects the perceptions others have of us.

Nonverbal communication can be obvious or subtle. Body language experts Patryk and Kasia Welowski say people convey unconscious emotions through "micro expressions" and that true feelings can be transmitted in as little as half a second.[5] Through nonverbal cues, we express feelings, disseminate information, reinforce messages, provide feedback, and exert control. We *encode* the information we send and *decode* the information sent back to us through body language.

In the U.S., it is generally agreed that hands clasped behind the back show confidence, clenched fists show firmness of resolve, a hand on the heart indicates a desire to be believed, and finger-pointing conveys aggressiveness or arrogance. Rubbing ones hands together equals anticipation, steepling fingers shows confidence, and hands in pockets indicates mistrust or reluctance. Hands folded in front indicate vulnerability, arms across the chest shows the person feels threatened, and talking with palms open suggests honesty. Smiles, laughter, and frequent eye contact signal friendliness and courteousness, head nodding shows empathy, and eye contact transmits credibility.

Note that nonverbal communication has different meanings around the world. Among the Japanese, smiles may indicate embarrassment, confusion, or discomfort. The A-okay sign means a variety of things in different countries—virtually none of them good. Unless we make a point to understand the meanings of nonverbal communication in other cultures, it is better to refrain from gesturing among international colleagues and clients.

Striking up a pleasant conversation is easier and less threatening if we first learn how to read others' nonverbal cues. It enables us to know when to approach others, when to keep talking and when to let others talk, how others are responding emotionally to what we're saying, and when to end conversations. If we see that someone is otherwise engaged in conversation, concentrating on a task, reading, eating, or praying, it's clearly not a good time to begin a conversation. However, if they smile, make eye contact, stand, nod their heads, look interested, or speak, they are conveying that they are open to an exchange.

READ THE CUES

- **If someone doesn't want to talk,** she will look away, frown, sigh, cross her arms, offer a quick furtive smile, keep her eyes on her device, or put up a physical barrier.

- **If someone is bored,** he will look around the room, check his phone, fidget, slouch, stand at an angle, avoid eye contact, sigh, roll his eyes, or have a vacant look.
- **If someone is angry,** she will narrow her eyes, lower her chin, purse her lips, raise a corner of her mouth, place her hands on her hips, glare, or point or wag a finger.

How close we stand to others is another means of nonverbal communication that is culture-specific. Americans feel most comfortable sitting or standing at an arm's length, but this distance would be considered too far apart among Middle Easterners and South Americans and too close among the Japanese. According to the life skills website, skillsyouneed.com, Westerners recognize four categories of distance: intimate, personal, social, and public.[6] When you violate those norms, knowingly or not, you make others feel uncomfortable.

KNOW THE DISTANCES

- **Intimate distance** ranges from touching to about 1.5 feet. This distance is reserved for close personal relationships, where eye contact and other nonverbal cues are not necessarily critical. This distance is too close for professional interactions as most will feel their space is being violated.
- **Personal distance** is somewhere between 1.5 feet and 3.8 feet. This distance is good for shaking hands or conversing with a friend or colleague. Depending upon the relationship, people may start at a lesser distance and move farther apart after introductions have been made. They may also move closer as the conversation progresses. This distance allows for observation of important nonverbal cues.

- **Social or professional distance** is anywhere from 3.8 to 11 feet. In this setting, the situation determines the distance at which to position yourself. If working on a project, you would be at the closer end of the range. If presenting at a meeting, the farther end is more appropriate.
- **Public distance** of 11 to 14 feet is used mainly by public speakers. At this distance, the subtlety of facial expressions is lost, which is why many public speakers rely upon expansive gestures to underscore their messages.

In conversation, note how far others stand from you. If you lessen or increase the space they will unconsciously move until their comfort level is restored. If you aren't sure how close to stand to someone, keep to the closer end of the social/professional distance range.

The Eyes Have It

Margot, new to the IT team, has outstanding credentials but her six-month performance review was mixed. There were no complaints about her work, but there were many about how she interacts with her team members. Margot, her team claims, is unapproachable, prickly, and dismissive. Teammates are afraid to interrupt her when she is on the phone or computer, and she is always on one or the other. This is a problem because they need to work together as a team.

So Margot is called into a meeting with Josephine, the HR manager, to discuss the matter. Josephine plans to ask Margot to assess her relationship with the team, thinking that if she recognizes her disconnect with her colleagues, the issue could be more easily rectified. Margot arrives, plops down in a chair, keeps her eyes glued to her phone, and says, "Okay, what's this all about?" Josephine tells her about the concerns voiced by her colleagues. She asks Margot if she can think of any areas in which she could improve her communication. Without taking her eyes off of her phone, Margot says, "That's ridiculous. I treat everyone respectfully. I don't know what they're talking about."

Josephine realizes this is going to be a much harder problem to solve than she had hoped.

When it looks like we are not listening, relationships may be at risk. We always need to decide what is more important at a given moment: connecting with the person in front of us or connecting with others virtually. When we make eye contact with others, we not only show respect and attention, we connect, build trust, and bond. Doctors, attorneys, and coaches use it to comfort, persuade, influence, encourage, and control. Without eye contact, they could not effectively do their jobs.

The extent and implications of eye contact vary from culture to culture. Among Asians, subordinates do not initiate direct eye contact with superiors, as it could be construed as disrespectful. In African and Latin American cultures, looking someone in the eye may be interpreted as aggressive or confrontational. In the Arab world, men engage in a high degree of eye contact, but consider it inappropriate between men and women. Britons engage in less eye contact than Americans, and Southern Europeans, more. When interacting with international business partners, it is important to remember these differences to avoid giving or taking unintended offence.

Eye contact does not come easily for everyone. Some find it threatening and others just find it uncomfortable. But in the U.S. and many other cultures, making eye contact is critical.

EYE CONTACT

- **Keep eyes up.** Do not look at other parts of the body. Gazes should be reflective of professional, not personal or intimate, relationships.

- **Make direct eye contact.** Hold someone's eyes for about five to seven seconds in conversation, look away for a few seconds, and then look back. He will know you are engaged without feeling under a microscope. If direct eye contact feels intimidating, look at the bridge of someone's nose or lower forehead.

- **Aim for eye contact 50 percent of the time.** It can be more when listening and less when speaking. Too much eye contact comes across as aggressive and too little, timid.

- **Practice, practice, practice!** Start with comfortable relationships, gradually moving on to acquaintances, passersby, cashiers, and wait staff. TV newscasters and even pets provide great opportunities to become more comfortable in making eye contact.

The Good Conversationalist

Darrell, a musician, was thrilled when he was asked to play for the President at a White House event. When he was informed he was welcome to bring a guest, Darrell immediately thought of Don, a longtime friend who had been involved in local politics for a number of years. The only thing was, Don was not a member of the President's political party, nor was he particularly a fan. Still, Don was not going to pass up an opportunity to go to the White House and happily accepted.

On the day of the event, Don thought he had never seen as excited a group of adults as those who were assembled to meet the President. When the President arrived, he spoke briefly to each person, and when it was his turn, gave Don his complete and undivided attention. Don knew he was briefed on the guests in attendance but was still amazed and flattered when the President referenced the alma mater they shared and asked Don if he had had a particularly demanding professor. He had, and they shared a laugh at how difficult his course was. They spoke for only a few moments, but Don left the event in awe, knowing he had been in the company of a great conversationalist.

Good conversationalists are polite. They know how to approach and join existing conversation groups. They know how to make smooth introductions and include everyone in conversations. They arm themselves with appropriate topics and steer clear of any that might be divisive or offensive. Good conversationalists know how to make seamless transitions from one topic to another, when to interject humor, and how to handle tricky situations such as conversational lulls or mistakes. They are good listeners and show interest in others. They do not argue, interrupt, or correct. Finally, good conversationalists know when it's time to leave a conversation group and gracefully move on.

THE COMFORTABLE CONVERSATIONALIST

- **Be polite!** Focus on others, not on your electronic device. Be present in the moment; don't look around to see who might be more important or interesting to talk to.
- **Join the group.** It's always easier when someone invites you into a conversation group, but feel comfortable joining one on your own. Never stand by yourself looking bored or

texting. Catch someone's eye, smile, extend your hand, and say, "Hello, I'm Joan Smith." Do not apologize for approaching a person or group at an event to which you were invited. It's your job!

- **Make introductions.** A good conversationalist is not shy about introducing herself. When making your introduction, offer a genuine smile, a warm, dry hand, full eye contact, and say your first and last name. In the social arena, age and gender determine the order of the introduction. Men are traditionally introduced to women and younger persons to older persons. In a social setting, you would say, "Mrs. Adams, may I introduce Mr. Phillips?" In a professional setting, rank is the determining factor, not gender or age. Persons of lower rank or power are introduced to persons of higher rank or power. You would say, using their real names, "John Client, I would like to introduce Ann Boss. Ann Boss, this is John Client." This order is followed because a client of any level outranks fellow employees of any level, even bosses and company presidents. After all, without clients, there are no companies!

- **Include everyone.** Make eye contact with everyone, even those who are not talking. They will feel part of the group and may be encouraged to join in. Ask for their opinions about the topic at hand or what brought them to this event.

- **Be prepared.** An experienced conversationalist knows the few seconds after an introduction can be awkward. Be ready with conversation topics to smooth the transition. When one-on-one, always be prepared to hold up at least 50 percent of a conversation. Tried and true topics like the weather, sports, or observations about the venue are always good icebreakers. Steer clear of risky topics such as religion or politics, or anything of a personal nature. Be creative! Eleanor Roosevelt would use the alphabet to get a conversation started. "Are you an art enthusiast?" or "Do you like baseball?" (Or cars, dogs, etc.) These will allow you, if need be, to break an awkward pause.

- **Cover up mistakes.** Ignore the mistake if you can: if you can't, downplay it. Say, "I do that all the time!" The person who made the mistake will be grateful, and you can immediately move on. If you made the mistake and it goes unnoticed, keep it that way. Otherwise, apologize or laugh it off and let it go.

- **Squelch inappropriate remarks or topics.** Tricky situations need someone to take control and smooth things over without causing embarrassment for the person who introduced the topic or for others in the group. If possible, pretend you didn't hear the comment, and change the subject. If necessary, be more direct, and say, "Can we talk about something else?" or "I'm sorry, I don't agree," or "I don't think that's appropriate." Then move on to a new subject—or a new conversation group.

- **Know how to move on.** Never monopolize others. The actual length of time you are in a conversation depends upon what you are talking about and with whom, but generally, be prepared to move on after about five to seven minutes. Say, "It was lovely speaking with you," or "Enjoy the evening," or "I hope we meet again!" Better to have ended a conversation with someone wishing it had lasted longer than having him regret he had to talk to you for so long!

The road to becoming a good conversationalist is bound to include some speed bumps. Keep trying. Most people won't even notice if you get a name wrong or mispronounce words. They'll be too concerned with the impressions *they* are making upon you!

The Power of Speech

Charlotte's organizational skills were unmatched. As executive assistant to the managing partner at an international law firm, she meticulously kept her boss's calendar, prioritized matters that needed his attention, scheduled his meetings, arranged his travel, maintained his correspondence, and screened his visitors. Charlotte researched information for her boss, as well as prepared spreadsheets, took meeting minutes, organized expense reports, reconciled charge card statements, made reservations, and bought and sent business gifts. When asked, she offered her perspective and gave advice. And on top of all of these responsibilities, she supervised the entire administrative staff.

Charlotte was perfect except for one thing. She had a dreadful telephone manner. She was abrupt with callers, including clients and board members, dismissive of staff, argumentative with vendors and service providers, and rude to solicitors. At best she had an imperious tone, at worst she raised her voice in anger to callers she thought had wasted her valuable time. But she never did any of these things within her boss's earshot.

And then one day, he unexpectedly walked into the office and heard her on the telephone. That was Charlotte's last day as executive assistant to the managing partner. She wasn't fired, but was immediately relieved of her responsibilities and demoted. In front of the whole staff she had treated so disrespectfully, she emptied her desk of her personal belongings into a box and carried that box out of the executive suite to a cubicle at the far end of the building.

The way you say something is far more important than the words themselves. Tone of voice conveys confidence, enthusiasm, respect, and interest, or the lack thereof. Pay attention to the delivery of your messages, because they can be easily misinterpreted and tarnish your brand in the process. Speaking patterns matter, too. Are you a high talker? A low talker? A fast, slow, loud, or close talker? Do you wander from the point or supply unnecessary detail and take too long to finish what you are saying? If you have ever gotten feedback about your speech, consider it a gift and take it seriously.

Keep in mind that it's possible you're getting feedback without realizing it. Do others often ask you to slow down, speak up, or repeat what you've said? Do they sometimes finish your sentences or supply words? Are you ever asked to lower your voice, either verbally or with a "keep it down" gesture? These are signals that indicate you may want to work on your speech.

Speaking too softly can make you come across as timid or unsure of your message. Speaking too loudly can make you seem aggressive. A very rapid rate of speech may indicate to others nervousness, overexcitement, or impatience. Taking too long to make a point may come across as someone who likes to hear himself talk.

Any of these speech patterns may annoy, frustrate, or cause concern to others. As such, it makes sense to try and modify them. Some characteristics are easier to change than others. But since strong communication skills are important for success, improvements are worth the effort.

SPEECH TWEAKS

- **Speak louder.** Think about what you want to say before you say it! Breathe from the diaphragm, and speak at an even, measured pace. Practice by reading aloud, and ask for feedback. Tune in to nonverbal cues. If others appear to be straining to hear, raise your voice, but do not shout.

- **Speak more softly.** Record yourself in conversation to determine your volume relative to others. Practice speaking more quietly. Strive for warmth and resonance in your voice. Speak less. Use nonverbal cues to relay your message instead of words alone.

- **Slow down your pace.** Enunciate each syllable. Have a clear message in mind, and speak in full sentences. Insert pauses, or "commas," into your speech. Control emotions.

- **Speed up your pace.** Read aloud and time yourself to get to a pace of about 150 words per minute. Introduce emotion into your voice.

- **Speak succinctly.** Employ an economy of words, and be as concise as possible. Make sure conversations are not sermons. Use appropriate vocabulary, not fancy words.

Professional resources are available to help you. Investing in voice coaching, improv lessons, or public speaking courses, such as those offered by Toastmasters, could quickly get your speaking skills up to par. Pulitzer Prize–winning American public affairs columnist William Raspberry said, "Good English, well spoken and well written, will open more doors for you than a college degree. Bad English, poorly written, will slam doors that you didn't even know existed."

Words still matter. Polite expressions that used to be commonplace and much appreciated are too often missing from many modern vocabularies. "You're welcome" has been replaced by "No problem," "Yup," or "Uh-huh." "I'm sorry" is now a shrug of the shoulders, an "Oh well," or a "What ev." "Hello" and "Good morning" are now "Hey," "How's it goin'?" or "S'up?" As always, the culture of the group dictates the norm, and if you are among coworkers who speak in a certain way, by all means feel free to join in. But generally, professional settings require more formal speech, especially if relationships are new, are one-time-only encounters, or involve persons from other countries. It is then best to err on the side of traditional politeness and offer a full-throated "Hello," "Thank you," or "I'm sorry."

When conversing with someone from another country, it is important to remember that the meaning of even a seemingly unambiguous word like *yes* is not universal. In some cultures, such as the Japanese, it is considered rude to say no. You may get a *hai* to something you say, but that only means someone hears or understands you, not necessarily that he agrees.

Mark Twain once said, "The difference between the right word and the almost right word is the difference between lightning and a lightning bug." Choose your words carefully, and use only those you can truly own. Know what the words mean, how they are pronounced, and the right context in which to use them. My friend mixes up common sayings so much that we've actually come to welcome and delight in them. This Ivy League graduate has notably said, "I'd swallow my sword for him" (fall on my sword), "Fair complete" (*fait accompli*), and "That's some beautiful blink" (beautiful bling). Among friends, such malapropisms can be funny and endearing, but business associates could be left wondering.

The words you use are an important element of your brands. Ban annoying terms, words, and clichés such as "touch base," "circle back," "deep dive," "value-add," "deliverable," "bandwidth," "synergize," "killing it," "socialize," and "low-hanging fruit." Resist peppering conversations with the latest slang. These words and terms can come across as unprofessional and exclusionary and are often dated within months. However, sites like onlineslangdictionary.com will keep you up on the latest, and allow you to understand the jargon. Avoid saying "utilize" or "signage" when "use" or "sign" work just as well. Steer clear of using words and phrases that made *Financial Times* columnist Lucy Kellaway's annual list of the "worst corporate guff." She said, "2015 broke all records for obfuscation, euphemism and ugliness." Examples included nouns used as verbs such as "to effort," "to language," and "to front burnerize," and euphemisms such as "ventilate" underperformers (fire), "bilateral telephonic meeting" (phone call), and "be careful of the optics of your personal brand" (tuck your shirts in).[7]

We all need to use good grammar. Saying "Me and Jim" instead of "Jim and I" will make colleagues who speak correctly wonder how someone managed to graduate from school and get a job without learning the basics of grammar.

In an article in CNN iReport, "Decline in Grammatical and Writing Skills of the New Generation Due to Techspeak," Fran Alston says the language, structure, punctuation, tone, and format used in communicating via electronic means, or "techspeak," is having a bad effect upon grammar. "There is a growing concern . . . among scholars who fret that the wide use of 'techspeak' is a real threat to the structure and real essence of languages."[8]

Electronic communication suffers most from the increase of "techspeak," but it has also crept into verbal communication. Commonly used terms and acronyms among millennials can leave older workers clueless. A useful resource for anyone who wants to learn or confirm the meanings of technology terms is "The Top 30 Internet Terms for Beginners, 2016" by Internet basics expert Paul Gil.[9] People can also consult sites such as con-nexin.net, onlineslangdictionary.com, and slang.org for help. Understanding the language of today's workplace will give digital immigrants more confidence in their interactions with younger coworkers. Digital natives need to be patient and helpful with older peers as they become conversant with new terms and acronyms.

Enunciation and regional accents are other aspects of speech to be conscious of. Speaking clearly, with as few fillers as possible (*um, ah, like, you know,* etc.), makes us sound far more articulate and thoughtful. Regional accents might require attention, too. Boston's "Paak the caah in Haavaad Yaad" is a real thing. Famous for dropping and adding *R*'s, Bostonians don't go to California; they go to "Californier." They drink "wata," not water.

Hearing an authentic Boston accent is, for me, comforting because it means home. But to people from other places, a strong Boston accent may sound provincial. If others can't understand you or tease you about your accent, try to minimize or even lose it if you can—or risk being seen as unsophisticated or unintelligent.

How do you lose a regional accent? Listen to newscasters! Their job is to disseminate information and build trust with the widest possible audience. To accomplish this, they must deliver news without a hint of regionalized accents. Try to emulate their speaking style by repeating their words with the same enunciation.

It goes without saying, using foul language or making disparaging remarks about others reflects badly on those using or making them. It could also cost promotions or jobs. Swearing raises red flags about an individual's maturity, self-control, and even intelligence. Foul language is offensive to many and can become an HR issue, especially if it is deemed offensive from gender, religious, or cultural perspectives. Swearing is tolerated in some industries more than others, but in general, using foul language does not enhance one's brand and may impact one's future.

The Good Listener

It's 8:00 Wednesday morning in Atlanta, and Zoe has arrived at her desk. There is an incoming call from her boss, MaryAnn, who is on an extended business trip to Tokyo. "Why is she calling at this hour? It's 9:00 P.M. Tokyo time!" Zoe says under her breath.

Then, like a ton of bricks, it hits Zoe: her boss is checking on the materials for this Friday's meeting—the materials Zoe hasn't sent! Before she left last week, MaryAnn had instructed her to FedEx to Tokyo 10 bound hard copies of the comprehensive proposal she would need for the client meeting, along with small gifts for each of the attendees. Originally, MaryAnn was going to carry them with her in her luggage, but with 10 days until the meeting, she decided it would be easier to have them shipped.

In her haste to get all of the predeparture travel details buttoned up, Zoe had only been half-listening to MaryAnn's laundry list of postdeparture instructions, thinking she'd deal with them later. Now, just two days before the meeting, there is not enough time to get the shipment to Tokyo. She braces herself and takes the call. She knows, too late, she should have listened more carefully. What could she possibly say to her boss now? She is filled with dread as she picks up the phone.

Listening is the great and rare gift you give to others. It shows respect and validates feelings. It allows them to vent emotions, gain perspective, clarify thinking, and develop trust. Listeners benefit, too. Greater understanding, fewer mistakes, improved morale, saved time, solved problems, and increased productivity are the results of good listening. Listening boosts reputations and strengthens career prospects. Listening is the magic bullet. So why don't people listen?

In part, it is because human beings have a limited attention span, estimated at just eight seconds. People are also so consumed by content on the Internet that they can barely remember their own birthdays, let alone the details of what others are telling them. It seems that an increase in the use of technology is met with a commensurate decrease in attention span.

The myth of multitasking is another barrier. Many people think they can effectively listen and engage in other activities at the same time. But there is zero evidence to confirm that. John Medina, author of the book *Brain Rules,* says, "The brain naturally focuses on concepts sequentially, one at a time . . . to put it bluntly, research shows that we cannot multitask."[10] Ryan Weaver, marketing analyst at Mentor Works Ltd., the financing consultancy, says "the proper word for what is commonly referred to as multitasking is 'task-switching,' and it is an imaginary skill."[11] No matter what it's called, studies point out that it doesn't work. When people try to perform multiple tasks at once, they decrease their productivity and increase their errors. And relationships suffer.

Short attention spans, multitasking, and a scarcity of time combine to make listening a challenging undertaking at best. Add to this the fact that most people are not all that interested in issues that do not directly impact them, and listening takes a hit. But listen we must! And it requires real effort.

Listening well means putting aside our own feelings and thoughts to absorb the speakers' thoughts and feelings. It does not necessarily mean agreeing with what others say, only that we *hear* what they say. Listening well means giving undivided attention, tuning into and mirroring others' emotions, relating as best we can to what is being said, encouraging speakers to say more, and paraphrasing often so speakers know they are understood. Good listeners don't push conversations in particular directions. Instead, they immerse themselves in what others are saying and feeling and then, if appropriate, share insights, answer questions, or offer solutions.

THE CAREFUL LISTENER

- **Remove distractions.** Give the person you are listening to your undivided attention. Turn away from your computer screen. Mute your phone. Look directly at the person speaking. And perhaps take the conversation to a private room to minimize interruptions.
- **Be receptive.** Don't judge what is being said, finish sentences, supply words, change the subject, or commandeer the conversation.
- **Provide feedback and convey empathy.** Emotionally connect with the person you are listening to and let them know you are interested and understand. Offer

conversational "door openers" such as "That's interesting, please go on" or "I'm glad you said that!" Tune in to their emotions by saying, "That sounds exciting!" (Or frustrating, confusing, overwhelming, etc.) Use nonverbal cues: nods, smiles, furrowed brows, or looks of surprise or delight.

- **Maintain discretion.** Loose lips sink more than ships. They can sink your business, your career, and your finances. They can even land you in jail. Gossip breeds ill will, poor morale, lost productivity, and permanently damaged relationships. Betray a confidence and people will see you as untrustworthy, unprofessional, insecure, or just plain mean. Conversely, the person who demonstrates she can be trusted wins friends and allies and gains a reputation as someone who is mature and professional.

As you advance in your career, the need for clear, sensitive communication will grow. Without strong communication skills, there may not *be* advancement. Warren Buffet, Richard Branson, Mark Zuckerberg, and Oprah Winfrey have followed different paths to success, but all are exceptional communicators. Each in their own way has learned how to engage in conversation, read and send nonverbal cues, and listen well.

REMEMBER

- **Nonverbal communication says volumes.** Read and use nonverbal cues to your advantage.
- **Eye contact has enormous power.** It shows respect, engenders trust, and helps strengthen brands.

- **Good things come to good conversationalists.** Practice your skills until conversation is one of your strongest skills.
- **Listening well reaps great rewards.** Use the knowledge and trust that respectful listening creates to become an exemplary employee, colleague, and business partner.

chapter 6

electronic communication

Smart Rules for Smart Devices

"Electric communication will never be a substitute for the face of someone who with their soul encourages another person to be brave and true."

—CHARLES DICKENS

Josh cannot live without his devices. What if a client emails him? What if his buddy texts him with playoff tickets? What if a cancellation gets him a table at that new Thai restaurant? What if his apartment application is approved? He's got to stay connected. Period.

But now, he is at this important meeting and they have all been instructed to close their laptops and put away their phones. Everyone quietly complies, including Josh, who tries not to show his irritation.

While the meeting drones on, Josh itches to look at his phone. He's been waiting all morning for a client's final decision on an important contract. "I'll just take a quick peek under the table," he thinks. Moments have passed, and now Josh, lost in reading all his messages, suddenly becomes aware of the dead silence in the room. He glances up to see all eyes on him. Josh quickly realizes that he has been called on to answer some question and that he never even heard his name called.

Red faced, he sheepishly asks, "Could you repeat the question?"

Now that we have mastered the art of face-to-face communication, we can exhale a sigh of relief and go back to the comfortable, controlled world of electronic communication. In the digital world, we're in charge. We communicate with whom we want, when we want, for how long we want, and by what means we want. In the digital world, we do not need to concern ourselves with the unpredictability inherent in in-person interactions.

Digital communication is, by great margins, the mode of choice for younger generations. Traditionalists still tend to favor face-to-face conversations when possible. Baby boomers like in-person encounters but do engage via telephone, email, and text. Generation X prefers email or text communication. Generation Y almost exclusively prefers text or social media. And Generation Z, the next on the workplace horizon, wants FaceTime.

These generalizations can sometimes be helpful, but it is a mistake to assume everyone in a category conforms to their generation's predominant communication style. My 90-year-old mother, a remarkably savvy digital communicator, regularly Skypes with her children and grandchildren, one of whom is her Navy pilot grandson in Okinawa.

You need to determine the best mode of communication for a given set of circumstances, and then undertake it skillfully.

Consider the means by which others prefer to communicate, and adapt to their preferred style. Think about what you're trying to accomplish, and then decide whether face-to-face, voice-to-voice, or text-based communication is the way to go.

Electronic communication disseminates information with speed, accuracy, and efficiency, but it is less effective in building relationships than face-to-face conversation. In his article, "Technology vs. Face to Face," Barry Siskind cites a report prepared by the *Harvard Business Review* comparing face-to-face communication with electronic communication. He concludes that in a number of key areas, including developing new relationships, negotiating, maintaining relationships, and overcoming cultural barriers, face-to-face communication beats electronic by overwhelming percentages.[1]

Telephone Skills

Mark has worked very hard to land his new position at a highly regarded graphic design agency, after graduating from one of New York's top schools. But now that he is on the job, some grim realities have settled in.

Mark presumed that work on actual projects would take up at least 90 percent of his time. He had failed to anticipate the incredible number of meetings, emails, and telephone calls every workday would include and the impact these would have on his project work. He is especially bothered by the lengthy, rambling email and phone messages he gets.

Mark was reminded of his college days when his mother would call and leave him long, detailed messages. Mark, most often, did not even listen to them and almost never called back. He had too much work to do. One day he got a call from his father, who told him that if he did not start returning his mother's calls, he would have to pay for his own phone plan. That got Mark's attention.

Mark's boss, a respected and tenured VP in the company, was now coming down the hallway. And he did not look pleased. His boss says to Mark, "I left you two urgent voicemail messages this morning about a client deadline that has been moved up. Why haven't you responded?" Mark was going to admit that he hadn't even listened to the messages, when his boss said, "In the future, I expect you to respond promptly. I would rather not have to walk to your office to get your attention." Mark starts to apologize, but his boss turns and walks away.

Mark now knows that listening to messages and returning calls is important, not just to his mother—it's important to *him* if he wants to keep his job.

Millennials would rather do anything—*anything*—than talk on the telephone. Or leave or listen to voicemail messages. They consider phone calls to be invasive, time-consuming, impractical, and "old school." Millennials so strongly prefer communicating through text and social media that many are not even sure how to leave voicemail messages. In his *New York Times* article, "At the Tone, Leave a What?" Teddy Wayne says, "Having grown up in a text-friendly culture, with unmediated cellphone access to friends, they [millennials] have had little formative experience leaving spoken or relayed messages over the phone."[2]

Many millennials just don't see the point of leaving voicemail messages. If a number shows up on someone's phone, that means that person should call back, right? The problem is, not everyone realizes this is an expectation. And even if they do, they are reluctant to return a call with no attendant message, thinking it could have been a misdial or "pocket dial." They may also not recognize the number.

It's not just millennials who have an aversion to talking on the phone; many of their older colleagues feel the same way. Once, the telephone was the only technology available, but now they too like the freedom and flexibility of text-based communication. Boomers and traditionalists will still usually answer the phone, but not always. Leaving a voicemail message was once second nature for them, but today even they do not necessarily like to do so. Like their younger colleagues, this generation has begun to experience a kind of performance anxiety and vulnerability. They feel a lack of control over how their messages will be judged—and whether or not their calls will be returned.

Despite all the talk about the lack of actual talk, telephone conversations may be experiencing a resurgence. People have begun to miss the sound of a human voice, the subtle nuances of tone, the intimacy, the clarity, and the immediacy. According to Jenna Wortham's *New York Times* article, "Pass the Word: The Phone Call Is Back,"[3] tech companies and entrepreneurs are introducing voice-centered mobile application services that strive to marry voice and convenience, the best of both worlds. The reassurance of a human voice, however and whenever it is heard, is once again in demand.

Collaboration is the predominant concept in today's workplace. Even as the tools of collaborative technology become more sophisticated, the seemingly old-fashioned methods of e-communication—telephone and email—are not going away. Industries such as financial services and insurance, among many others, still rely heavily on cold calling to conduct and solicit business. Companies also rely on the well-honed telephone skills of employees in call centers to attract and retain business, and to guard the reputations of their brands. Even the largest e-commerce companies in the world, including Amazon and eBay, need telephone representatives to step in when technology falls short in meeting their customers' needs.

Remember switchboard operators? Those cheery-voiced humans who knew how to quickly and correctly route calls and actually made callers feel that they appreciated their interest in their organizations? They still exist, but in rapidly declining numbers. The position of a switchboard operator, or company telephone operator (actual switchboards haven't been used since the 1960s), may soon be extinct. Now direct-dial extensions, automated systems, and the occasional receptionist handle all incoming calls.

Still, it's trickier than ever to actually get someone on the phone. If callers can even find a company's phone number, they will often reach a recording encouraging them to visit the company's website because "we are experiencing heavier than normal call volume." A caller is required to navigate a maze of recorded options, all with further options of their own, to finally get to the right person or department. Those making business calls increasingly find people won't answer unless the calls were agreed to and scheduled in advance. An impromptu call is now often considered inconvenient, intrusive, and even inconsiderate.

Business Calls

When answering or placing a business call, you have one chance to set the tone for a relationship. Since up to 70 percent of a phone message is conveyed in tone of voice, it's not what you say—it's *how* you say it.

- **Answer professionally and enthusiastically, ideally by the second ring.** Offer a greeting, "Hello" or "Good morning," followed by the company or department name and your full name. Put a smile in your voice. If callers identify themselves, refer to them by their name and add "Mr." or "Ms." Use first names only if invited.

- **Use good grammar, speak clearly, listen well, and give the call your undivided attention.** Others will know if you are reading, typing, or otherwise distracted. Do not eat, drink, or chew gum while on the call. Be aware of background noises.

- **Ask permission before placing someone on hold, and wait for an answer.** If it is a lengthy hold, come back within a minute to update the caller on the status of your behind-the-scenes efforts.

- **Show politeness, patience, and respect unfailingly, regardless of the caller's demeanor.** A call is often precipitated by a problem. If a caller is upset, let him speak. Apologize for his inconvenience. This does not mean you are necessarily accepting responsibility for the problem, but simply acknowledging he is upset. Often, this is all that is needed to diffuse emotion and get the conversation on a positive track.

- **Treat every call as important.** Sometimes you won't know until after the fact just how important a call or caller was.

Placing calls reflects on your brand and your company's brand, too. When initiating calls:

- **Organize your thoughts before the call.** Make sure you identify yourself. If the person was not expecting your call, assess her tone of voice. It will convey her openness to speaking with you. Asking if your call is convenient at this point allows the person the choice of continuing the conversation. This, on its own, often relaxes the recipient enough to continue. If it is not a good time, ask when would be a better time.
- **Leave enough, but not too much, information on voicemail.** Speak clearly and slowly. Leave your name and number at the beginning of the message and at the end. Do not leave ambiguous or personal messages or bad news on voicemail.

Have you noticed that virtually no one returns calls anymore? If a call is not a cold sales call, the reasons are myriad. It could be that the caller failed to leave a recognizable name or intelligible number. It could be that the recipient is away, consumed by work, or never listens to messages. It could be that whatever precipitated the call, such as following up on an inquiry or proposal, has been put on the back burner by the recipient. It could also be that someone is no longer interested in pursuing the conversation or business relationship and, rather than being up front about this, just hopes the caller will give up and go away.

Whatever the reason, it is confusing and disheartening when a call is not returned, especially if there is a preexisting business relationship or the other person initiated the dialogue. Try not to take it personally. You may follow up once and maybe even twice, but after that, it is better to let it go. Relentlessly pursuing someone not interested in communicating at that moment does not generally strengthen a relationship. Instead, focus on other projects. Oftentimes, the person will circle back to you when the timing is right.

If you are the one who initiated a dialogue or requested a quote, proposal, or information, it is courteous to return follow-up calls or emails. Even if your answer is "no" or "not now," you will have respected the other person's time and preserved a relationship that you may need or want again in the future.

Cell Phones

There are officially more mobile devices in the world than there are people, now numbering upwards of 7 billion. As mobile phones—cell phones, satellite phones, and smartphones—continue to proliferate, the opportunities to bother others while using them do too, at an equal pace. We have all probably been guilty of a mobile phone faux pas at some point. If so, it may be time for a phone self-intervention.

CELL PHONE SELF-INTERVENTION

- **Keep mobile phones off of meeting tables.** Otherwise, others will presume that it is only a matter of time before the conversation is superseded by an incoming call or text. Known as "phubbing," short for phone snubbing, this practice bothers people. Kelly McGonigal, author of the *New York Times* article "The Willpower Instinct," says, "Research shows just having a phone on the table is sufficiently distracting enough to reduce empathy and rapport between two people who are in conversation."[4] Among business or social peers, keeping your phone out may be acceptable, but among clients or higher-ups, it is better to put it away.

- **Do not use a mobile phone at a business, social, or family meal.** Excusing yourself to the restroom every 10 minutes or texting under the table are obvious tactics to circumvent this rule. In some circles, phone use at restaurants has been drastically curtailed by dining companions who agree to put their phones in the center of the table: Whoever answers a call or text first pays the bill!

- **Use a phone in social situations only if it benefits the group.** If you need to get directions, make reservations, call a cab, clarify a point, or get a sports score in which everyone is interested, use your phone. If your group's culture allows for phone use, feel free. But do not be the first, as a domino effect will quickly take hold.

- **Do not use a mobile phone in a church or a synagogue,** or at any solemn occasion such as a wake or memorial service. Do not use a phone in a doctor's office, at the movies, at the gym, in a locker room, at parties, or while ordering or checking out. And of course, no texting while driving or walking. In 2015, a woman was hit when she walked into the path of a freight train while texting. Miraculously, she survived.

- **Take photos only with permission** and never with unsuspecting persons in the background. These may end up on a public feed, which would be an invasion of their privacy.

Telephone Options

Andrew would have preferred the Quiet Car on his Amtrak trip from New York to Boston. But since he will probably need to answer a couple of calls, he chooses Business Class. This way, he can take any necessary calls and still enjoy the relative tranquility Business Class typically affords. When Connor boards in New Haven, Andrew quickly realizes today's trip would not be typical.

Once seated, Connor, a guy with cockiness to spare, immediately gets on his devices and puts his phone on speaker so he can have both hands free to type. At a decibel level the entire car can hear, Connor's conversations include a litany of complaints about his demanding employer, his difficult client, and his complicated love life, replete with individual and company names.

Andrew is uncomfortable. And from the body language the other riders are exhibiting, he knows they are as well. So he decides to ask Connor if he would please lower his voice and take the call off speaker. Connor looks at Andrew. "If you want quiet, go to the Quiet Car," he says, making a dismissive gesture as he continues his loud conversation.

Speakerphones

Speakerphones are great for hands-free phone conversations, but they can be uncomfortable for those at the other end. If a conversation is between just two people, a headset is a better option, as it allows for both convenience and privacy. However, once you are hands-free, the temptation to multitask can be overwhelming. If you are prone to this temptation, it may be better to pick up a handset.

At work, a respectful, productive speakerphone meeting follows a pattern. After securing a private room, the meeting leader begins the call by asking permission to put someone on speaker. She then introduces others in the room, or asks them to introduce themselves. Throughout the call, participants identify themselves before speaking and speak at normal decibel levels. If anyone leaves or joins the call midway, the person on speaker is always advised. The call is given undivided attention by all participants, who refrain from holding side conversations, eating, or using other electronic devices. The meeting leader wraps up the call and thanks everyone for attending.

Conference Calls and Videoconferences

All of the guidelines for speakerphone calls apply to conference calls. Because conference calls are generally more formal and involve more people, they require some additional guidelines as well.

Conference call organizers send invitations with all pertinent call-in information and agendas in advance and reminder notices the day before and/or morning of the call. If there is a service provider, they test all technology beforehand so there are no problems on the big day. Agendas include all items that will be covered and who will be responsible for addressing them. If there are primary speakers on the call, it will include their bios.

Attendees prepare for the call by completing any assignments or reading indicated, and by jotting down questions and points they would like to raise. Participants call in at least three minutes before the scheduled start time, using reliable phones to avoid dropped calls. When the organizer has not muted the call, attendees mute their phones and check to be sure they have actually done so. This is an especially important point for those working from home offices, where distractions abound.

Participants stay focused, adhere to the agenda, and bring ancillary matters up after the call. It is tempting to do any number of other things during a conference call, from answering email to running to the restroom. But that is to be avoided, as invariably that will be the very moment the call participant is asked for his input.

Videoconferencing, or real-time audio/visual communication between or among individuals or groups, is the technology of choice for companies wanting a solution for cost-effective collaboration. Videoconferencing requires all of the preparations and precautions of speakerphone and conference calls, but since participants are now seen, attention to nonverbal cues becomes important as well. Whether they are sitting in a conference room or a home office, participants will take great care with their attire. Since everything is on display, they will make sure furnishings and décor reflect professionalism. Spaces will be uncluttered, artwork will be tasteful, accoutrements will be appropriate. Overflowing wastebaskets, crammed bookshelves, and bobblehead figures will be out of sight.

Email

Annabelle has her hands full. As assistant athletics director for a Division One college, she is responsible for special programs for student athletes. She also meets with a fair number at the behest of their coaches for individual instruction. There are more than 30 teams, and with an otherwise full schedule, Annabelle's calendar is jammed every day of the week. Still, she is happy to give of her time to those who need extra guidance.

What makes Annabelle less happy are some of the attitudes she encounters. Even though their coaches have required them to meet with Annabelle, she sometimes feels like they think they are doing *her* a favor. She received an email from a student athlete with the subject line empty, no salutation, no closing, and no context. In its entirety, it read, "Hi when do you want to do this."

Complaints about email are deafening and universal. In-boxes full of messages with missing subject lines, misspelled words, improper grammar, inappropriate language, and indecipherable acronyms are just some of the grievances. A succession of "Reply All" messages is the biggest complaint. In some organizations, real-time group messaging apps such as Slack, which eliminate the dreaded "Reply All," are replacing internal email. Group-messaging apps are quickly catching on and may eventually become standard for internal communication. But they will still require adherence to guidelines for professionally written email.

According to the Radicati Group, the technology market research firm, email is still the go-to form of business communication. Email Statistics Report indicates:

- The number of business email accounts will reach 1.1 billion by the end of 2017.
- The number of business emails sent and received per user per day will increase from 122 in 2015 to 126 in 2019.
- Email addresses are still required to access IM and social networking sites and are also needed for online transactions such as banking and shopping.[5]

Despite all of the other ways to communicate, work email is going to be with us for the foreseeable future. This is not good news for many millennials, who look at email much like voicemail: something to be tolerated until it finally dies. Millennials are often perceived as being unable or unwilling to write professional emails; indeed, many have not written a full sentence since they were in school. As a result, the quality of millennials' writing skills is considered one of their biggest impediments in getting jobs, and once on the job, in getting ahead.

All generations are at the mercy of carelessly crafted, hastily sent emails. Nancy Flynn, founder and director of the electronic policy training and consulting firm ePolicy Institute, says a lot of people don't realize that "email creates the electronic equivalent of DNA. There's a really good chance of emails being retained in a workplace's archives, and in case of a lawsuit, they could be subpoenaed."[6]

A lot is at stake as seemingly bright people learn the hard way every day. Professionals at the highest levels in their fields have lost their jobs, ruined their reputations, and suffered extreme personal, financial, and health consequences as a result of carelessly crafted, hastily sent emails.

You can avoid these problems by, first of all, never *ever* emailing when angry. It may feel good for a moment, but remorse and all its ugly ramifications will quickly set in. If you simply must vent, do so with a trusted companion—your dog or cat maybe—or write your complaint out in longhand and then throw it away. Do absolutely anything but electronically communicate anger. It will become part of your permanent digital dossier.

Unless there is no other way, do not use email for highly personal messages such as those about illness, death, divorce, or pregnancy. These are emotionally charged messages, better shared face-to-face or at least voice-to-voice. Be extremely careful of the content of professional emails. If your company is ever sued, your emails could become part of e-discovery, the process of gathering ESI (electronically stored information) for legal purposes. Apply the standard of "if you would not say it face-to-face, do not write it in an email." Studies show that people are much braver when communicating from behind a screen and that the lack of nonverbal cues makes typewritten messages sound much more aggressive than intended.

EMAIL GUIDELINES

- **Use the subject line to summarize the focus of the message.** Incorporating "URG," "REQ," or "FYI" lets recipients know if the email requires immediate attention, a request is being made, or information is simply being conveyed. Double-check email addresses before hitting the send button. Send only relevant emails to those who need to receive them.
- **Do not send "Reply All" or "CC All" messages unless absolutely necessary.** Use the CC field if someone needs to be privy to an email but does not need to respond. Use the To field if a response is requested from the recipient. Use BCC (blind carbon copy) ethically, and not to mislead that an email exchange is confidential. Protect others' email addresses, contact information, and messages by not forwarding them without their permission.
- **Read through email threads completely before responding or forwarding.** Once our names are attached, it is a tacit admission that we have read them. Before writing, determine how formal the email should be based upon the relationship with the recipient. Greater formality is in order with clients, company executives, persons from cultures

where formality is valued, and those we do not know well. Apply business letter–writing standards by including an appropriate salutation and closing. Make sure sentences are properly structured and words are correctly spelled. Observe the rules of capitalization and punctuation.

- **Allow words to convey their meaning and emotion.** Steer clear of emoticons and emojis in professional emails. Avoid using all capital letters, no capital letters, multiple exclamation points, bold typeface, bright colors, or flashing text. Also avoid marking every email "high-priority" or using RR (Read Receipt). Recipients find these annoying.

- **Proofread all emails.** Use but do not rely solely upon grammar check and spell-check. Read emails aloud to be sure they reflect the intended tone. Do not send or forward jokes, chain mail, political or religious messages, virus warnings, fund-raising appeals, or inspirational sayings. If forwarding an email, edit out all extraneous information and include a brief personal note. Be concise and brief and make one main point. I know of one executive who on principle will not read past two lines in an email. Use bullets.

- **Respond to emails promptly.** If you cannot respond at least by the end of the day, have an "out of office" message automatically sent back to the recipient.

Hardware

Freelance marketing consultant Evelyn loves the flexibility and comfort of her home office. And she is thrilled she no longer needs to fight the rush hour traffic that made her commute so grindingly stressful, a commute she had made for years. Still, it can be lonely.

That's why the nearby coffee shop Evelyn discovered came to be a sanctuary for her. Perfect for freelancers like herself, it was never too crowded or noisy and always had friendly, familiar faces behind the counter and at the tables, too. Evelyn could get her work done while enjoying freshly brewed coffee and low-key fellowship with others whose workdays were organized similarly to hers.

This truly was, for her, a little piece of heaven. But lately, a new clientele has upset the welcoming feel of the shop. There is a man whose music is so loud that even with his earphones on, Evelyn cannot concentrate. Another man watches movies at full volume, compounding the situation. Then there is the college student who takes up two tables and four chairs for her coat, papers, and all her electronic devices. Finally, there is the woman who purposely overhears Evelyn's conversations and then comments upon them! It's just not the same anymore.

Evelyn is reluctant to give up the coffee shop, but already several of her acquaintances have stopped coming. Evelyn is pretty sure she will be next.

In public places, consideration for live human beings always takes precedence. When listening to audio on a laptop or tablet in a public place, use headphones to avoid disturbing others. Sometimes it is okay to physically spread out a little, but during busy times, be aware of space constraints and adhere to the rule of one chair and one electronic device on a table per customer. With regard to public Wi-Fi, remember that public bandwidth may be limited; save the downloading of huge files or the watching of movies for home. Also, remember that public networks are by definition less secure. Use a virtual private network (VPN) service for a secure Internet connection.

The Message

Barbara realizes that things have changed considerably in the nearly 25 years since she joined the hospital as an X-ray technician. She still loves her work and welcomes the advances in technology that help her do her job better. And she delights in mentoring new hires as they come through the department, even though she could, now, be their mother. Their energy and enthusiasm are infectious and keep her on her toes.

One thing Barbara is having a hard time getting used to is the way younger folks communicate. It's like they are speaking a foreign language. Take today's text from a new employee, Ava, who Barbara is helping on a project: B- JTLYK, will be l8; h8 traffic! F2F ASAP? Project FUBAR! TY, SYS!

Not wanting to admit she is completely lost, Barbara goes online to research the meaning in the message. Aha! Ava just wants to let Barbara know that she will be late as she is stuck in traffic, which she hates! But when she gets to work, can they have a face-to-face meeting as soon as possible? The project Ava is working on is fouled up beyond all recognition, and Ava would be very grateful for Barbara's help. She will see her soon!

Acronyms and Abbreviations

Since the essence of text-based communication is brevity, some acronyms and abbreviations *may* be okay as long as the reader readily understands what the writer intends and the message is appropriate. In business emails they should be rarely used, as such shorthand could come across as unprofessional. But professionals still want to be familiar with the most often used communication shortcuts. There are a number of excellent sources for Internet jargon, including netlingo.com and the *Internet Slang Dictionary*. A visit to one of these sites will get you up to speed with ICYMI, EOBD, TL;DR, AFK, and NSFW (especially) in no time!

Texting

Despite its foibles—wretched autocorrect and messages that go astray, get sent too soon, or are indecipherable— text messaging, or SMS (short messaging service), is still immensely popular. Yes, it has lost ground among the 18–24 age group to apps like WhatsApp and Snapchat, but texting is still the go-to among business professionals. When communicating by text, the urgency of the message should be taken into consideration. Some people see and read their texts immediately, others not for hours or even days. If in doubt, it's safer to call.

TEXTING TIPS

- **Consider whether a text is the best mode of communication with a particular person.** Even if you have your boss's number, a text might not be her preference. However, if she texted you in the past, and the information is appropriate, then feel comfortable using this medium. If someone sends you a text, reply in kind, instead of with a phone call. When a text exchange gets lengthy, it is appropriate to suggest a phone conversation to speed things up. With group texts, include only those who really need to see them.

- **Spell words out in professional texts.** Use punctuation even if it seems laborious and unnecessary. If using the voice-to-text feature, carefully review the text before sending it, as it may read nothing like what you intended. Tone, humor, and sarcasm can be easily misinterpreted via text; use these sparingly.
- **Do not walk and text; never drive and text.** The Centers for Disease Control and Prevention says that each day 9 people die from distracted driving and more than 1,000 are injured.[7]
- **Allow others to respond as they can.** Do not send successive follow-up texts or a snarky "Anyone there??" Be aware of the timing of your text. On the West Coast, you may still be at work at 8:00 P.M., but your East Coast business partner who sleeps with his phone next to him will be awakened by your text.

Instant Messaging

Instant messaging is real-time communication between individuals via the Internet, similar to a private chat room. IMs are practical for internal communication, especially when collaboration is desired. But it is not a perfect solution for everyone. Many find IM intrusive yet do not want to disable it for fear of missing important messages. The rules of good grammar, tone, professionalism, and brevity apply to IMs as they do for all text-based communication.

IM GUIDELINES

- **Do not, generally, send IMs to strangers.** Some people do not mind and actually solicit them, but others consider them presumptuous. Ask how someone wishes to be contacted. Use a greeting before launching into your message, and ask if the IM recipient has time to chat.
- **Use and respect status messages.** If someone has set her status as "Do Not Disturb," then do not disturb her!
- **Use acronyms carefully.** Acronyms are slightly more acceptable with internal IMs, but when in doubt, spell it out.
- **End an IM exchange with a sign-off.** Rather than run the risk of leaving someone hanging, end with a "Thank you" or "It was nice talking with you" message.
- **Address one point at a time.** Wait for a response before moving on to the next point. If your message must be divided into multiple thoughts for the sake of clarity, insert a line break between each thought. For a lengthy exchange, it may be better to ask if the person has time to talk.

The Company Intranet

When used respectfully and thoughtfully, the company intranet provides an efficient platform for internal communication and collaboration. Employees use the intranet to internally crowd-source ideas and gain feedback on initiatives. Used effectively, the company intranet supports a corporate culture, disseminates information, and enhances productivity.

- **Learn your organization's intranet "Dos and Don'ts."** The system administrator may have a formal document and colleagues can also quickly get you up to speed.

- **Determine if you are ready to have a document reviewed or commented on.** In some organizations, once a document is saved on a shared platform, it is fair game for anyone's comments and edits. Never pass off someone else's content as your own.

- **Keep your user name and password secure.** Do not store sensitive information, including pin numbers, credit card numbers, and bank account numbers on the intranet.

The ways in which you can communicate and collaborate will only become more sophisticated over time. It won't be long before holographic telepresence technology allows for in-room communication with real-time, full-motion, 3-D images of colleagues continents away. As technology continues to develop at a breakneck speed, it can seem overwhelming. If you remember to practice the Platinum Rule, you will be just fine.

REMEMBER

- **Text communication will never equal the power of the human voice.** Developing telephone skills is time well spent.

- **Email continues to be the go-to means of business communication.** Professionals are judged by their email practices and the content and tone of their messages.

- **Human beings take precedence over electronic devices.** Attached as we are to them, we must look up from and put down our devices.

- **Professionalism never takes a holiday.** Appreciate the speed and convenience of text and instant messaging, but never forget that text-based communication lives forever.

chapter 7

twitter, etc.

Acing Social Media

"Technology is a good servant but a bad master."

—GRETCHEN RUBIN

D rew and Will, both 22 years old, have spent their entire lives together. They grew up in the same town, went to the same schools, worked together at the same summer jobs, and are now graduating from the same college. In a few weeks, they will start new careers: Drew heading off to a top tech company in California and Will to a plum financial services job in New York City. It's bittersweet to go their separate ways. But tonight they will celebrate!

They wrack their brains to come up with the perfect setting, when it dawns on Drew that his family's best friends have not yet left for the summer for their beach house by the shore. Every year, his family spends time at this beautiful waterfront home. These friends have even invited Drew to stay weekends on his own, trusting him so much that they let him know where they keep the spare key.

"This will be perfect!" Drew thinks. They will "borrow" this lovely beach house for just a few hours, and no one will be the wiser. And they will be ultracareful. Drew shakes off any reservations; he is, after all, practically a member of the family. They wouldn't *really* mind. So Drew and Will text their friends on the drive down to the shore, inviting them to a low-key gathering and emphasizing *low-key.*

In the blink of an eye, what they envisioned as a small gathering of friends turns into a raucous melee of 100 people. Beer, wine, and food are spilled on the furniture and rugs. Couples are in the bedrooms upstairs. The kitchen is a disaster. Soon inebriated partiers begin to post the festivities on social media. Sure enough, someone, a neighbor, recognizes the house and alerts the owners.

Police cars arrive at the scene, and Drew and Will spend the night in the county jail. The next day, they stand in front of the judge, lawyers quickly assembled, with parents, the friends whose home they used, and a reporter from the local newspaper. They face a total of 23 counts, including charges of breaking and entering and reckless endangerment of minors. Drew and Will, hands shaking, enter their pleas: "Not guilty, Your Honor." A court date is set—three weeks *after* they were to jet off to their new jobs and new lives.

Social media have revolutionized the business world. As recently as 2003, Facebook, LinkedIn, and Twitter did not exist. Now, they are so much a part of our daily lives that we scarcely think about how new and world-changing these technologies are. At this writing, the largest platform is Facebook, followed by YouTube, Reddit, Twitter, Pinterest, and Instagram.[1]

Snapchat is also huge, especially among those under 34 and the savvy companies marketing to them. Live video streaming, such as Twitter's Periscope app, is also gaining momentum, as are podcasts. All sites share cyberspace with countless more focused on every demographic and interest imaginable.

Your Digital Footprint

A social media devotee since its beginning, Sarah keeps up with her numerous friends, some going all the way back to junior high school. All through her 20s and now early 30s, Sarah has shared the big moments of her life online—her college graduation, engagement, wedding, travels, jobs, and the most cherished news of all, the arrival of her children. She has loved learning about all of her friends' milestones as well. Sarah can't imagine her world without social media and wonders how her parents' generation survived without it.

Now, with family, work, and volunteering, Sarah is busier than ever before. It occurs to her that she has lost track of all of her sites and her activities on them, especially those from years ago. She's always been careful with what she shares, but now that she is in management, she wonders if there is possibly something lurking in her past posts that would not fit her image today. She doesn't think so, but decides it's better to be safe. Tomorrow, she will do a thorough social media review.

Personal and organizational digital footprints are growing larger by the second. With every post, visit, share, tag, like, snap, and forward, social media users leave traces of digital DNA that can never be erased. The chilling implications of this fact have resulted in an increased interest in the "right to be forgotten," a controversial topic involving the removal of Internet search results containing incriminatory information about one's past. It is a complicated issue with freedom of speech, information integrity, and censoring implications that will likely not be resolved any time soon. In 2014, Google lost a battle with the European Court of Justice over failing to comply with their ruling on this matter. Regardless of how the issue is ultimately resolved, you would be wise to heed Jeffrey Rosen's warning. In his *New York Times* article, "The End of Forgetting," he says, "It's not just that the web and social networking threaten your privacy. It's that there is no way in the digital age to move on, to start over—to erase your digital past."[2]

There is a lot at stake in your use of digital technology, including your safety, security, reputation, relationships, finances, credit worthiness, insurability, and employment. In real life, if you are lucky, the mistakes you make may be forgotten. Online, mistakes live forever. There is no way to reset your reputation, no way to declare "digital bankruptcy," no way to start over. And transparency, a good thing in relationships and business dealings, has a price online. The worst thing you've done will be the first thing someone finds when they search your name.

The list of bright, successful people who have gotten into trouble on social media is very long. All we need to do is read or watch the news on any day via any medium to learn of yet another prominent person going down in flames due to ill-considered online activities. These missteps often cost them everything. Others survive them, but only after offering public apologies. Companies are also not immune to social media gaffes, and many highly regarded organizations have had to do extensive online damage control. With so many cautionary tales, and the widely held feeling that by now we should know better, it is a wonder that this is still happening. Still, for many, the temptation to vent online is irresistible.

Social media also pose serious potential dangers for companies. Data loss, security breaches, compliance violations, reputation damage, compromised intellectual property, and leaked strategy initiatives are some of the risks. CNBC's Mark Fahey says one of the most costly consequences of social media misuse is lost productivity. In his article, "Time Wasted on Facebook Could Be Costing Us Trillions of Dollars," he wrote that time spent on Facebook alone is costing employers $3.5 *trillion* in squandered productivity.[3]

Realization of the potential impact of online transgressions is increasing. To help manage their online brands, some individuals and organizations are hiring reputation repair and management companies, often for a hefty fee. These companies try to bury, not remove, unsavory online articles and references. They also monitor social media for new problematic items that might pop up.

It is possible to fix a less-than-perfect digital dossier without investing enormous amounts of time and money. And a great deal can be done for free. First, start with an online audit. Even if you've done one in the past, content constantly changes without your knowledge, consent, or control. If any new questionable tweets, photos, or videos are discovered, delete them, and ask friends to do the same. Second, consistently add new content to bury potentially damaging items. According to Dorrie Clarke, a marketing strategy consultant, "No one but your worst enemy will bother to visit page 20 on a Google search; most will stick to the first page or two."[4] Videos rank high on Google searches, so she advises including a video blog to ensure that people see what you want them to see. She also recommends a traditional blog and a robust social media presence, including profiles on LinkedIn, Facebook, and Twitter.

Keep in mind that it is far easier to make a good impression online than it is to unmake a bad one. Protect yourself by not airing personal grievances or angry opinions, no matter how justified you might feel, or posting anything that could be considered racist, sexist, or any other "ist" you can imagine. Never engage in online shaming, a dreadful practice often equated with cyberbullying. Make sure all of your online content is relevant and useful, and apply the same standards for virtual communication that you use in real life. This means listen more than talk, respect others' opinions, apologize for mistakes, avoid arguments, express appreciation, and always be accountable.

Businesses are very much aware of the reach and power of social media. With upbeat stories and positive news items, they seek to attract followers and build relationships through "social selling." Their ultimate goal is to convert leads into clients, and clients into brand advocates. But like personal users, businesses are not immune to costly social media failures. Companies that have tried to disguise online promotions with "sympathy" for national tragedies and natural disasters have paid dearly for their greed and insensitivity. Human error is also an ever-present risk. Ryan Holmes, CEO of Hootsuite, wrote about a particularly embarrassing tweet sent by a major international brand, when an employee unknowingly linked an X-rated photo to a response to an unhappy customer. It went to the company's entire Twitter following and stayed up a full hour before someone noticed and took it down.[5]

To expand their reach, companies are increasingly tapping into their employees' social media networks, positioning themselves to take advantage of the enormous marketing potential these offer. Studies show that millennials especially are far more influenced by online endorsements made by their friends than they are by direct marketing from brands. Companies that use their employees as brand ambassadors must be careful because they are at risk by association. Many are implementing social media training programs to help employees understand their organization's social media strategies, online best practices, and the benefits to them of being brand ambassadors.

Companies need to avoid heavy-handed approaches. Employees cannot be coerced into offering up their networks, nor can there be any infringement on their rights to free speech under the National Labor Relations Act.

Even as professionals learn the basics of social media, they will continue to educate themselves in their use. When Jon Thomas, director of strategy for advertising agency TracyLocke, is asked why a pristine social media presence is so important for professionals, he says, "As publishing becomes increasingly ubiquitous, where anyone can share their thoughts on their own blog, on Medium.com, LinkedIn, YouTube, Facebook, or even in 140 characters on Twitter, the idea of a résumé encapsulating the identity of a professional is rapidly becoming outdated." He added, "Sure, I can dig through your résumé and listen to your answers in an interview, but if I can understand how you think and approach your profession from what you publish online, I can get a much clearer picture of your approach to our business, and more importantly, what your impact might be on our business." Esta Singer, digital media specialist and founder of the social media consulting firm, s.h.e. CONSULTING, says a "social media presence means you don't need to work at being found online. You've built a positive reputation by building strong relationships, posting timely and relevant information, engaging followers, and demonstrating integrity. Having an online presence means you are able to demonstrate and share value."

There is still a percentage of the working population that, for reasons of privacy, safety, personal preference, or the risks described, chooses not to use social media. But if a professional is not searchable, especially on LinkedIn, it immediately begs the question "Why not?" or "What is he trying to hide?" Today, social media is where the business conversation takes place, with or without us. We need to be part of the conversation.

The Cyber Citizen

In a moment of self-reflection, Edward wonders how he got so mean and judgmental. The 55-year-old senior executive at Class A Spaces, a leading commercial real estate firm, has mentored countless young folks over the years. He was always happy to do so and has taken great pride in their accomplishments. Edward credits his own success to his mentors and the amazing network he built over 25 years in the business.

Things are so different now from when he started. Back then, networking was done face-to-face over business meals and after-hours drinks and at conferences and sporting events. Edward has always loved those in-person connections and knows the relationships he developed from them are largely responsible for his success. Today, networking is almost all electronic. Edward understands the time-saving appeal of mass-networking, but is not as sold on the value or quality of some of the relationships that come from it.

Take LinkedIn. On any given day, Edward receives multiple invitations to connect, the majority of which come from people he doesn't know. Most of the invitations are impersonal and seem hastily sent. All are blatantly self-promotional, about what *he* can do for *them*. To be honest, he isn't inclined to do anything for them. It's difficult to endorse people who have unprofessional profiles or share strong political or social views. His credibility is at stake. It's hard for him to reject these invitations even though that is his inclination. Edward again wonders just how and when he became so mean and judgmental.

The ever-changing and ever-growing number of social media platforms makes it unfeasible to learn the individual best practices for every one of them. The good news is you do not need to. Adhering to basic guidelines for use with all media is almost all that is required to keep your brand intact. It is important, however, to learn the differences between the major platforms, as each has its distinct purpose and personality. When you want to clearly understand what should be shared on a specific site, think first of the three Ps: whether the information is suitable for *public*, *private*, or *professional* audiences.

Even when using platforms as intended, you need to discern the fine line between being appropriately social and inappropriately *annoying*. We all have the "friend" who cannot go one day without posting yet another cloying platitude, detailed description of her awesome life, or cat video. Observe what happens on the various platforms. Social media offer swift, often stinging feedback. Sometimes just *not* doing as others do is all that is required.

We have identified respect as the basis for all personal and professional success. There is no place where respect, or the lack of it, is more starkly displayed than on social media. The reach, speed, and permanency of behavior on social media can literally make or break a career. Online respect is not only a good thing, it is also imperative for workplace survival.

On social media, respect starts with adopting the attributes of a good cyber citizen. In his book, *Unmarketing*, Scott Stratton describes the concept of "social currency." He says if one wants value from social media, one *has* to first build currency.[6] Once someone has proven to be helpful, his network will be more willing to help in return. Like a bank, you can't make a withdrawal until you have made a deposit!

Respect your privacy and others' privacy. A teacher was fired simply because someone else posted a photo of her having a beer at a bar while on vacation. Be considerate about what you share on your own and on your friends' pages and feeds. If a message is at all personal, send it to the person directly.

Very important: Never post anything that could jeopardize the safety or personal property of yourself or others. This means you do not share anyone's home address, current location, or travel plans. It is estimated that 80 percent of burglars glean information from social media to plan their activities. Criminals employ Google Street View to stalk homes, view Facebook to monitor check-ins at hotels and airport lounges, and use location data garnered from posted pictures to know when someone is not at home. Users themselves often openly advertise and chronicle their comings and goings via posts and photos, giving thieves extremely useful information.

You can avoid being a victim of "cyber casing" by not sharing upcoming travel plans online, not checking in from remote locations, and not posting photos until you are home. Keep your phone from giving away your location by disabling geotags and GPS tracking and by not publishing photos directly from your phone.

Online best practices require that you consider how your friends' posts reflect on you. If their posts often include inappropriate language, photos, or humor, it may be time to rethink these connections. Some worry that to "unfriend" someone on Facebook, especially if he is a family member or longtime friend, will do irreparable harm to that relationship. Luckily, privacy settings allow for stealth ways to limit what people see without having to blatantly unfriend them. These include "hiding" people from your feed, using privacy features to customize what others see, and turning off chat features with particular friends or blocking them. You can, of course, actually unfriend people, too. They won't be notified, but will probably figure it out.

All major social media platforms have privacy settings and sharing features. These differ from site to site and seem to constantly change, making it hard to keep up. Staying current with and using sites' privacy settings are the best ways to protect your brand and relationships.

First impressions matter online, as they always do in life in general. Regardless of the platform, always introduce yourself; don't assume others will know who you are. When inviting someone to join your network, include a brief, warm, personalized note, not the generic message provided by the platform. In completing your professional profile pages, use an actual photo of yourself at the age you are now. Your baby photo, *however* cute, can be confusing and possibly seen as inauthentic or unprofessional. On all sites, use good grammar and check your spelling.

Just as in real life, you choose your friends in cyberspace and they choose you. Sometimes you receive connection requests from people you do not know or from people you *do* know but do not wish to connect with. You do not need to accept every request nor will all of your requests be accepted. Many people have strict guidelines for themselves about whom they will accept as connections. Some will just connect with immediate family, others with extended family and close actual friends, and others with anyone who invites them! Don't take it personally if your request is not accepted. Some think it is rude to ignore friend or connection requests; others think it more humane to let them sit in pending mode rather than reject them outright. Who knows? In the future, you may want to connect with this person. It may be better not to burn a bridge.

The intervals at which you post may also reflect upon your social media savvy. SumAll, a data analytics company, offers these posting guidelines: Facebook, two times a day (more than that, and likes and comments will drop off); LinkedIn, one time a weekday; Google+, three times a day; Twitter, three times a day; Instagram, up to two times a day; Pinterest, up to five times a day; and a blog, up to two times a week.[7] But social media guru Esta Singer says there is no magic number and that the "frequency depends upon your audience and relevance of the information you are posting." Your posting intervals will likely vary depending on what's happening at any given moment in your life or in your connections' lives. The bottom line: Good judgment is key, as you may be judged by your posting frequency.

The Social Network

At 65 years old, Stephen is a Facebook novice. For years, his out-of-state daughters had been asking him to set up an account so they could share photos and videos of his grandchildren and generally stay up on one another's lives. Stephen used to think Facebook was for kids, but now most of his friends have accounts. So he finally decided he would take the plunge.

But it's been hard for him to get the hang of it. Wall posts, status updates, timelines, messages, lists, privacy settings—it's all overwhelming. And boy, is he making mistakes. Yesterday, he sent a long message to an old friend he recently reconnected with, catching him up on 20 years of his life: relationships, work, health—it was all there. Stephen soon got a private message back from his friend. "Did you really intend to post on my timeline?" his friend asked. "I don't know . . . I *think* so . . . why?" Stephen wrote back.

His friend explained that timeline messages are visible to all of *his* friends and that in the future, he might want to share these messages privately. Lesson learned—the hard way, thinks Stephen.

A scenario like this is unthinkable to digital natives, but to those just getting their feet wet in social media waters, it happens all the time. Digital natives have an edge over their older colleagues with regard to social media etiquette, mostly because they wrote the rules! As this technology evolved, they learned which behaviors were acceptable and welcomed on the various platforms and which were not. Now that guidelines have been widely agreed on and adopted, later social media entrants can quickly get up to speed with a little research and a lot of good judgment.

As a card-carrying digital immigrant, I reached out to my network, which includes some folks who make their living in social media. These experts vetted my advice and shared their own best practices for the most popular social media sites. Meant to be a primer, the following may be brand new information for digital immigrants or a review for digital natives. For those who live and breathe social media, it will serve as a simple reminder of the importance of practicing good habits.

Social Sites

Fifty-eight year-old Christine, CEO of a large apparel company, has so far resisted the pressure. Christine has heard from her executive team how important it is for her to have a social media presence and about the benefits to the company of a CEO who is seen as accessible, transparent, and responsive. But the few spare moments she has after her typical 80-hour workweek she wants to spend with her family, not tweeting or posting updates on LinkedIn. Besides, it just seems complicated and too risky. Christine has seen other executives get into big trouble and have to apologize for their online mistakes. And although she would never tell this to her team, in her opinion all of this "sharing" is a bit beneath the dignity of a CEO.

Still, she pays her executive team to give her this kind of advice, whether she likes it or not. She asks her assistant to arrange some time with the PR Department to get her set up. She is going to need their help.

Facebook

Facebook is a social networking website that enables users to join networks of friends, family, and people with similar interests. A Facebook profile is one's personal account on Facebook. Here, people can "friend" others, post photos and videos, "like" and share others' posts, send messages, and provide updates. Depending upon privacy settings, a user's friends may see a user's posts on his "wall" and have the ability to comment on his posts. Only one Facebook profile can be associated with a name. While not a business-oriented site, Facebook has implemented a feature that allows users to add professional skills to their profiles, increasingly leveraging its users' vast social connections to compete in the job search market.

In his article for *Yahoo Tech,* "11 Brutal Reminders That You Can and Will Get Fired for What You Post on Facebook," Dan Bean shares these stories:

- An employee posts, "I hate my boss," and gets the comment, "You do realize we're friends on fb, right?"
- A young intern says he cannot come to work due to a family emergency. He shows up the same day on Facebook in a photo at a Halloween party, dressed as a wand-wielding fairy.
- An employee posts " . . . so happy to be listening to T4F, while pretending to work," and gets the comment, "We are the people who pay you while you pretend to work. Please come and see me."
- A young man posts a photo of himself doing drugs and gets the comment, " . . . give me a good reason not to fire you first thing Monday morning."[8]

In contrast to a profile, a Facebook page is a business account through which brands ask customers and prospects to like their pages to follow their brands. Here, they can also advertise with Facebook ads. To have a Facebook page, one must first have a Facebook profile. However, one can then have as many pages as he desires. It's important to keep personal and business connections and profiles separate. One reason is that use of a personal account to promote a business is against Facebook's terms of service, which may result in Facebook deleting the account. Equally important is that content shared on personal and business accounts is, or at least should be, meant for distinctly different audiences.

A Facebook page is a great way for a business to grow a following, establish credibility, and measure engagement results. It's important to take time to learn best practices for this medium and to remember that it's a two-way conversation. All comments, both positive and negative, require a response.

When using your personal Facebook account, it is recommended that you "friend" only people you actually know and like. But for many users, younger people especially, it is still a "more friends the merrier" scenario. On average, those in the 18–24 age range have 649 Facebook friends.[9] Interestingly, *U.S. News and World Report* cites an Oxford University study that says of all our Facebook friends, only four are *actual* friends—the same number we have in real life.[10] When deciding upon how many Facebook friends you want to have, it is wise to remember that the greater the number of Facebook friends, the greater the risk of information falling into the wrong hands.

ANNOYING HABITS

- **Spamming.** Soliciting, promoting, or selling of any kind is considered spam. On Facebook, most people are fine with requests for donations to charities or personal causes, but draw the line at crowdfunding requests for leisure travel, a sabbatical in Provence, or a new boat!

- **"Vague booking."** Posting intentionally ambiguous updates can come across as narcissistic or passive aggressive. Posts like "NEVER again . . ." or "This can't go on . . ." cause concern and/or irritation among friends.

- **Providing TMI.** Too much information includes photos of recent surgery scars, 50 vacation photos, or a baby's naked behind. If you must share, be extremely selective about who sees these posts.

- **Jeopardizing others' privacy.** As proud as parents are of their children, by posting their photos and activities, they are making privacy and safety decisions that could have lifetime implications for those too young to consent. The advice is to think carefully about what and how often you post about others, especially children. In France, parents can now be sued by their adult children and possibly jailed for having posted their photos on social media without their permission.

- **"Humble bragging."** The practice of packaging good news as though it's actually an inconvenience is both obvious and insufferable. "Our Billy just got accepted at Harvard and Yale. Poor thing, now he has to decide between his dad's alma mater and his mom's!" Actual bragging gets old, too. Facebook is for sharing one's happy news among real friends and family members, as long as such posts do not dominate and self-congratulation is kept at bay. Promoting friends' good news is great, provided it's someone you actually have a relationship with in real life. Otherwise, it can seem creepy. But if the good news is about you or an immediate family member, allowing friends to share it whenever possible has a much nicer ring!

There are some everyday Facebook practices that can help us avoid potentially sticky situations. They include making sure we send private messages for two-way communication, refraining from posting status changes unless all affected parties have been notified (a young man learned his parents were divorcing when he saw that his mother had changed her status to single), and being careful about checking in from Starbucks when we are supposed to be home sick! But perhaps the easiest way to make sure our Facebook friends actually stay our friends is to subject our posts to these three filters: Is it interesting? Is it helpful? Is it entertaining? If our posts meet these criteria, we'll stay a welcome Facebook connection.

LinkedIn

A LinkedIn user recently garnered an extraordinary number of comments when she posted a picture of herself in a bikini, admittedly and purposely to gain attention. It worked, but judging from many of the comments, not in an entirely favorable way.

LinkedIn is a business-oriented social networking website for professional summaries, industry-related groups, networking events, and career marketing. It also has messaging functions that allow users to post status updates and to share or like content posted by others. As of August 2016, LinkedIn had 450 million members worldwide.[11] In June 2016, Microsoft acquired LinkedIn for $26.2 billion. Said Microsoft CEO Satya Nadella, "Think about it: how people find jobs, build skills, sell, market, and get work done and ultimately find success requires a connected professional world."

While there are now networking sites that cater to professionals of all stripes and at all stages of their careers, LinkedIn is still very much the premier destination. With newer features that seem to have a distinct social slant to them, many users are beginning to lament what they consider the "Facebookification" of LinkedIn. An increasing number of nonbusiness-related posts including the sharing of personal stories, political views, and even one's availability for dating are putting the site's professional status at risk.

Some see this evolution as a sign of the times, a reflection of the melding of personal and professional lives, and not necessarily a bad thing. Why *wouldn't* individuals want to take full advantage of their entire networks? As features of the largest social media sites become more commonly shared and the major sites themselves increasingly indistinguishable, this cross-pollination may indeed be the way of the future. But for now, most feel drawing a distinction between how personal and professional sites are used is a good thing.

To protect the value and integrity of your relationships on LinkedIn, most say to connect only with people you have actually met. Others say it's okay to connect with people you do not actually know if you have other people in common or share professional interests. If you do not know someone personally, request an introduction or explain who you are and why you want to connect. Referencing that you heard someone speak, or read and enjoy her blog, or share an alma mater may just garner you a new connection.

BEST PRACTICES

- **Take advantage of vanity URLs.** They are easier to remember and more personal. Write a professional summary/bio. Be honest on your profile. Former colleagues and bosses will note embellishments and inconsistencies. Complete your LinkedIn page, and update it regularly. An old or abandoned page raises red flags.
- **Ask for recommendations only of people who are familiar with you and your work.** Reciprocate recommendations whenever possible. Endorse others for their skills as you see fit and thank others for their endorsements.
- **Accept invitations promptly.** Unless you have a good reason not to accept an invitation (you do not know someone, or you do—but think he would not reflect well upon you), accept an invitation when it is received.
- **Join groups and associations to harness the expertise of your fellow LinkedIn members.** Be sure to read and then follow the group's rules. You can certainly start your own group but make sure you are able to commit to it.
- **Avoid excessive self-promotion.** Examples include using groups or associations to promote your services or content or posing a problem and then answering it with a promotion of you or your company.

Twitter

Susie Poppick of *Money* shared a story about a city clerk in California's Bay Area who she said was asked to resign for "allegedly tweeting during council meetings when she was supposed to be taking down meeting minutes." The woman resigned, writing in her letter that it was a "mind-numbingly inane experience I would not wish upon anyone."[12]

Twitter is a social networking and micro-blogging service that enables its users to send and read messages known as "tweets." Tweets are text-based posts limited to 140 characters displayed on the author's profile page and delivered to the author's subscribers, who are known as followers. Other Twitter users may also view tweets unless the author specifically elects to limit dissemination of tweets to followers only. As of June 2016, Twitter users could also post 140-second videos.

Twitter is different from other social media in that there is no acceptance process for followers of your feed. It is possible to protect your tweets, but that will limit the business and networking benefits you seek. Some people argue that you should follow everyone who follows you and use lists to keep track of those you truly care to follow. You are under no obligation to follow someone who tweets content that is of no interest to you or is obviously self-promotional, regardless of whether they follow you or not.

Esta Singer offers her perspective on the importance of this site to professionals: "Twitter is akin to a worldwide social gathering. You're meeting and mingling among people you know, have met, or will meet. You're having conversations, and sharing ideas or information you think could benefit others. Most importantly, you are building relationships. Be authentic. Be transparent." She adds, "There is an etiquette to Twitter most of us have already learned: extend a virtual hand, offer something of value, say 'thank you' when someone shares or re-tweets your tweet. While the Twittersphere is ever-expanding and endless, always be mindful, it is not about the quantity of followers you amass, it's about the quality of connections you create."

BEST PRACTICES

- **Remember this is a two-way personal communication tool.** Add more value than you request. Social media guru Chris Brogan offers this guideline: "Promote other people 12 times to every 1 self-promotional tweet."[13] Don't ask for re-tweets. Contribute relevant and interesting content and it will be re-tweeted.

- **Create a list of Twitter accounts you truly care about.** Too many, and it's hard to keep up. Make sure your bio is complete with a photo, full description, and link to further information about you. An incomplete bio is a sign of a spammer.

- **Keep Twitter exchanges brief, not more than three each way.** After that, use a more practical means for communicating, such as email or telephone. Use the @ symbol for talking directly to individuals in moderation. Following long @ exchanges can quickly become tedious for the others not involved in the exchange.

- **Use the hashtag (#) sign to make content, conversations, and trends searchable.** Long a staple on Twitter, it is used to categorize subjects, find related content, and gain wider audiences. The hashtag has been criticized for its overuse and, as such, should be used thoughtfully. This means not overloading posts so the subject itself is indecipherable and not using long, cryptic hashtags.

- **Be extremely careful of the messages you post.** If you must address a private matter, do so via direct message (DM), not in front of your entire Twitter audience.

Summary

As you traverse the ever changing, tricky terrain of social media, commit to learning as much as you can about the unique characteristics of the various sites. Do take the social media plunge even at the risk of making mistakes. Keeping in mind the basics of *authenticity, transparency, respect,* and *relevancy* will keep you on the right track.

REMEMBER

- **Social media has changed the world.** Engage in ways that favorably burnish your brand, and you will be considered credible, competent, and current. Be consistent on platforms.
- **Digital footprints are forever.** Personal reputations and company brands are at risk through social media misuse. Take precautions to mitigate these risks.
- **Social media benefits are incalculable.** It's a matter of making the decision to join the online conversation.

chapter 8

business dining

Observing the Formalities

"If you ever have to choose between 'advanced accounting for overachievers' or 'remedial knife and fork,' head for the silverware."

—HARVEY MACKAY,

author of *Swim with the Sharks Without Being Eaten Alive*

For a month, Miguel had been planning what he hoped would be the perfect visit to Boston for his biggest client and his wife. He arranged for them to be picked up in a limousine at the airport and whisked off to the exclusive Boston Harbor Hotel, to a luxury suite with a view overlooking the Boston skyline. Knowing his client loved lobster, Miguel made reservations for the best table at the famous Legal Harborside on Boston's waterfront. To cap off the evening, Miguel arranged for a private harbor cruise.

Miguel planned their next day with the same meticulous attention to detail. He knew his client's wife loved Asian art and arranged for a private docent tour of the Asian art collection at the Museum of Fine Arts. Afterwards, they made their way to historic Fenway Park for a Red Sox game. The special day ended with a late dinner at Mistral and a box of Montecristo #2 cigars for his cigar-loving client.

Miguel's preparation paid off. Everything came together to create an impeccable experience. Impressed, his client told Miguel it was "the best weekend he and his wife have ever had" and that he looked forward to a long, mutually beneficial partnership. It was a perfect ending to the perfect weekend, just as Miguel had hoped for.

Alas, Miguel's business dining and entertaining experience was one that few ever *actually* experience. Because there are so many moving parts with client entertainment, something is bound to go wrong and almost always does. Guests arrive late or not at all. Reservations go astray. Crowded, noisy dining rooms hinder conversations. Kitchens get backed up. Service is slow. Wrong or incorrectly cooked meals arrive at the table. Servers are surly. Glasses topple, silverware falls, and food flies. Guests argue or over-imbibe. And all of this happens before the credit card is declined. And these are just the business meals. Every other client entertainment vehicle has its own inherent potential perils.

Business dining is rife with risk, but it is a risk the serious professional wants to take as often as possible. You can expand opportunities, acquire information, garner advice, gain introductions, and strengthen bonds, all for a pittance in the investment of time and money. Business dining is the perfect vehicle for welcoming business partners, celebrating good news, rewarding major milestones, showing gratitude, delivering apologies, and sharing important or difficult news.

The savvy professional knows a business meal is not about the food. In calm and comfortable surroundings, away from the frantic pace of the office, a guest is far more likely to let her genuine persona emerge, laying the groundwork to establish true rapport.

The Business of Hospitality

Jack, head of sales for a financial organization, had been looking forward to his company acquiring a significant piece of business. They had had serious competition but, still, he was confident they would ultimately win the deal. So, after months of pursuit, it came as something of a shock when he learned they did not.

When Jack asked the president what the decision had rested on, he was assured that the problem was not his company's proposal, which was very competitive in all areas.

"It was a tough call," he told Jack. In the end, it was the social relationship the other company had created and the pleasant, easy rapport they had established. The climax was a magnificent formal dinner they arranged for his company's entire executive team and their spouses. "They not only wined and dined us," he said, "they made us feel like family."

Every detail of the dinner had been meticulously planned. The spectacular view from the top floor allowed guests to see a setting sun as it melted into the evening twilight and intermingled with the candle-lit tables, all reflected off of floor-to-ceiling windows. And then there were the quietly beautiful place cards—minor works of art, with each attendee's name handwritten by a calligrapher.

The president believed that if this was the level of preparation and respect he and his company could expect as clients, this was the place for them. "Those place cards closed the deal," he told Jack.

Breaking bread in business has always been about strengthening relationships. And it is as important today as it's ever been. But a dedicated dining experience outside of the office for the purposes of building a relationship is out of sync with the way millennials do things. It makes no sense to them, especially when they can grab fruit, yogurt, or a Kind bar from the office kitchen and keep on task. Why pay for food and drinks when their employers offer them for free? Relationship building for this cohort is done across the open-plan office or via social media, not at formal place settings. Traditional business entertaining is becoming less of a priority to older generations as well.

This is shortsighted. The significance of hospitality has a long history, dating back to the first recorded writings some 5,000 years ago. One reference of this was found in the Teachings of Khety, c. 2100 BCE:[1]

> "Give the stranger olive oil from your jar,
> And double the income of your household.
> The divine assembly desires respect for the poor
> More than honor for the powerful."

Throughout history, hospitality was the means through which generosity, honor, and respect were shown. It serves the same purpose in the 21st century.

Globally, the significance of business dining and entertaining cannot be overstated. A critical component of establishing trust, business dining in the international arena determines whether or not there will *be* a subsequent business relationship.

The *Financial Times* has a wonderful, semi-regular column in its magazine, *How to Spend It,* called "The Captain's Table." In this column, they interview extraordinarily successful businesspeople about where in the world they most like to dine and their thoughts on the business dining experience itself.

Richie Nanda, executive chairman of the international security firm Topsgrup India said, "I would say that 80 percent of my business is, in some way, conducted over lunch and dinner. I am very much into relationships, and believe that to form good ones and conduct successful business you need to be relaxed—and that often comes as a result of enjoying a good meal on a one-to-one basis."[2] Joseph Sitt, president and CEO of Thor Equities, a global portfolio and development pipeline, says, "My mentor, an Egyptian businessman called Joseph Chehebar, once told me 'If you don't have a meeting set up over a meal that day, then don't come to work.'"[3]

In the U.S., entertaining of clients often *follows* successful business dealings, but around the world, they are integral throughout the *entire* process.

International dining customs vary widely, and serious professionals go to great lengths to prepare themselves accordingly. They know that when dining with Japanese clients, you never pour alcohol for yourself. Among Arabs, you do not use your left hand to eat, as that hand is considered unclean. Attire, introductions, gift-giving, conversation, dining etiquette, the significance of alcohol, toasting, and after-hours entertainment are just some of the important elements that are carefully researched before dining with international business partners.

In the U.S., if we entertain at all, it is often for practical reasons. We are busy and our clients and colleagues are busy, but we want to meet, and we have to eat. So we opt for the "two birds with one stone" approach and convene over a meal. This may seem an efficient tactic, but may also leave a great deal of potential on the table. Working breakfasts and luncheons are perfectly fine if billed as such up front. And, of course, if clients want to talk business over meals, we are happy to comply. But if stronger alliances are what we are after, we need to let the balance of conversation be about nonbusiness items.

While you are learning about your dining companion over a business meal, you too are under the microscope. Your guest is on the lookout for clues about you—your personality, your integrity, and how much you value this relationship. The amount of thought you give to the choice of venue, the invitation, the greeting, and the seating of your guest are also under evaluation. How you interact with the server, order wine, steer the conversation, deal with the unforeseen, and pay the bill are, too. At a business meal, your grace, generosity, and personal characteristics are on display and contribute to your guest's evaluation of you and your overall suitability as a business partner.

Business dining opportunities involve more than just those with clients and prospects. Coworkers, employees, and bosses get to see us eat every day. And the people who hold our professional futures in their hands notice us as we wolf down our overstuffed Italian subs, our chins dripping with olive oil.

Business dining is also a big part of the interview process, especially if the job will include face-to-face client interactions. A prospective boss does not invite a candidate to lunch or dinner because she thinks he is hungry. Her concern is how this person would fare in an unscripted and unpredictable social situation that may require any combination of good judgment, flexibility, humor, kindness, and consideration.

Walt Bettinger, CEO of Charles Schwab, the brokerage and banking company, uses the business dining experience to evaluate how well job candidates deal with adversity. In an interview with Adam Bryant of *The New York Times*, he said he takes candidates to breakfast, arrives early, and asks the server to deliberately mess up the candidate's order. "That will help me understand how they deal with adversity. Are they upset? Are they frustrated? Or are they understanding? Life is like that and business is like that."[4] He says it gives him a window into their hearts, not just their heads.

Prospective employers are also carefully observing how comfortable candidates are in sophisticated surroundings, how appropriate are their choices of food, drink, and conversation, how aptly they display dining skills, and whether they glance at their electronic devices. A false step in any of these areas could cost an otherwise qualified candidate a job offer.

One might agree that dining skills are important, but question whether the lack of them is an issue. It is. We have mentioned that one of the biggest obstacles millennials face in the workplace is their perceived lack of social skills, dining skills among them. Many think that the decline in teaching manners, traditionally done at home, began in the 1970s as women began to enter the workplace in greater numbers. Scheduling demands put the family dinner on the back burner, so to speak. As a result, the basics of how to use silverware and engage in respectful conversations, and why the telephone is *not* answered during the meal, went untaught. But if this theory is correct, it is not only millennials who missed out on these important lessons—a fair share of their older colleagues may have as well.

Hosts and Guests

Bill didn't really mind that his guest had picked out the restaurant. It was his city after all, and he knew the best places. And Bill thought as long as his prospect was happy, the better the chances their relationship would get off to a great start.

When Bill gets to the restaurant, he takes a peek at the menu. The prices are eye popping! Still, that was okay because this guy seemed like the real deal. His guest arrives and, after a bit of small talk, Bill invites him to order. "Okay," he says to Bill. Then, to the server, he says, "I'll start with a dozen oysters, then the Caesar salad, and the prime rib, rare." After a momentary pause to mentally calculate the bill so far, Bill asks his guest if he'd like wine. "Sure," he says, asking the server to "bring us your best bottle of Cabernet."

Bill tries in vain over dinner to engage his prospect in conversation, each time only to be met by the man chewing a mouthful of food and gulping his wine. When dinner is finished and dessert offered, the client asks for the menu once again. He orders not just dessert, coffee, and an after-dinner drink for himself but, to Bill's astonishment—dinner and dessert to take home to his wife!

The long evening finally nears its end and the check comes. As Bill reaches for his wallet, the client crumples his napkin into a ball and says to Bill, "Great dinner—thanks! My wife's gonna love this," holding up his wife's take-home dinner order.

In delving into the subject of business entertaining, a good place to start is with the responsibilities of hosts and guests. Unlike the social arena in which such roles are not always defined, in business they generally are. And both factions need to know their responsibilities to play their parts accordingly.

Before an invitation is extended, a host must know why she is extending it. Being clear on what a host hopes to accomplish will inform all decisions to follow. Next is the choice of venue. Perhaps the occasion is a quick introductory or information-sharing meeting, where coffee at a local cafe or even the company cafeteria works well. Maybe it is a more leisurely get-to-know-you luncheon, where a quiet venue is the best choice. It could be a celebratory dinner, where nothing short of a five-star restaurant with an excellent wine list will do.

When selecting a venue, the host considers her guest's convenience, comfort, and taste. If the guest's food preferences are not known, the host opts for a restaurant with a wide assortment of popular foods. Most restaurants that cater to business clientele have selections that appeal to all comers, including vegetarians, pescatarians, carnivores, vegans, and the gluten-free. Some quick online menu research will reassure a host that her guest's preferences, whatever they are, will be accommodated. A host does not, however, ask the guest to choose the restaurant. This puts undue pressure on the guest to discern what level of hospitality the host has in mind and what her own food preferences might be. But the host can suggest different kinds of food, for example, Japanese, Italian, seafood, steak, etc., to get a sense of what her guest might like.

It's always a good idea for a host to scope out the prospective establishment before taking a valued client or prospect there. Are the food and service top-notch? Is the noise level acceptable? Does the table spacing allow for a private conversation? Is the décor tasteful? Is the menu understandable? Knowing that the venue will be suitable in all regards gives a host confidence and allows her to focus on the building of the relationship.

Once a venue is selected, an invitation is extended. Usually, a telephone or email invitation will suffice, but for a formal event such as a ceremony or banquet, a printed or engraved invitation may be in order. The formality of the event also dictates how far in advance an invitation is extended. For casual meals, it can be as short as a few days; for special occasions, it should be at least three weeks before, perhaps preceded by a "save the date" announcement.

On the day, the host arrives early, ready to greet her guest. If the guest gets there first and does not see his host, he may be concerned about having gotten the day, time, or place correct. Or he may just wonder why the host isn't there—not a question a host wants a guest to ask. A host checks her guest's coat and keeps the ticket to retrieve it later. The maître d' escorts the guest to the table, and the host follows the guest. Once at the table, the host invites the guest to be seated in the best seat, which could be the one with the beautiful view or the most comfortable-looking chair. The guest sits to the right of the host at a table for four. If it is a table for two, they sit across from one another.

Immediately upon sitting, the host removes her napkin from the table and puts it in her lap. Menus will be presented after which the server, or ideally the host, invites the guest to have something to drink. If the guest accepts and chooses a drink containing alcohol, the host also orders a drink, although it does not need to be alcoholic. Having familiarity with the menu, the host makes suggestions to the guest, including some selections from the high end of the menu's price range. This allows the guest to feel comfortable ordering without concern for price. If the guest does order lobster or Kobe beef at the host's suggestion, she is prepared to order something commensurately expensive to relieve him of any concerns about being extravagant. Once the meals have been selected, the host offers the guest wine to accompany the meal. If there are two people dining and only one drinking wine, or if different kinds of wine are preferred, it is perfectly acceptable for diners to order wine by the glass. Otherwise, it is up to the host to order wine by the bottle. After the drinks arrive and the meals have been ordered, it's time to get down to the business. The business of building a relationship, that is.

Throughout the meal, the host stays in complete control. She interacts with the server as needed, keeps the conversation going, handles any difficult situations that might arise, constantly anticipates her guest's needs, and ends the meal gracefully. She has already made arrangements with the server or maître d' to hold the check rather than present it at the table, sidestepping any possible awkward discussion about splitting the tab or leaving the tip. The meal over, the host escorts her guest from the restaurant, retrieves his coat, tips the coat-check person, and walks the guest to the front door. There, if a cab is needed, the host either hails one or tips the doorman for doing so.

When the host is a woman and the guest a man, or the guest is considerably older than the host, complications can arise. This is because some men and some older people feel more comfortable in the role of host. Both men and women want to guard against behaviors that hint at gender distinctions, and all want to avoid presuming that the older person automatically pays the bill. To ensure there is no question about who is hosting, one lets the server or maître d' know upon her arrival that she is the host. The staff will then proceed accordingly, deferring to the host and guest as appropriate in their respective roles.

There are many things over which we have no control at business meals. Preparing for the inevitable hiccups, literal or otherwise, that are just part of the dining experience allows us to go with the flow. Staying calm, ignoring what we can, tactfully handling what we must, and laughing off the rest is the best approach. No matter what happens, it is truly never the end of the world. And who knows? It may even end up being a bonding moment!

What has the guest been up to while the host has been orchestrating this impeccable dining experience? Ideally, he has been displaying exemplary dining skills and enjoying this wonderful hospitality. A good guest knows this is his host's show and does not usurp her responsibilities in any way.

The Mechanics of a Meal

Frank is ravenous. He comes to this business conference every year, mostly because they always host dinner at the best steak house in the city. He looks forward to this big, delicious dinner more than any other part of the conference.

Seated at the table, he grabs his napkin and gives it a big flap before tucking it under his chin. Now ready, he orders a gargantuan steak, to be broiled to his specifications, and a double order of thick-cut fries, golden and crisp, just the way he loves them! He holds his knife and fork, clenched in each fist, as though he were going to carve the beast himself.

In his mind, there is nothing better than this. Except, darn it, they always ruin things by bringing broccoli. Frank sure as heck is not going to let this broccoli get in the way of his perfect steak dinner. So he takes the bread off of his bread plate and puts it on the tablecloth. He then tips his dinner plate and pushes all the broccoli florets on to the empty bread plate.

There, problem solved.

First impressions always begin with limited information. There is the tendency to think that if someone is skilled in one area, say quantum physics, they are also skilled in another, say basic utensil-holding. If the person is not skilled at holding a fork, the thinking goes, how can he possibly be trusted with subatomic particles?

First Impressions

When there is a large group of attendees at an event or formal dinner, there may be a receiving line to allow attendees to meet the host and guest of honor. Since all eyes are on the VIPs in a receiving line, it is important to avoid boisterous behavior in line. Keep your right hand free for a handshake, and move quickly through the line. Next, it is time to meet and mingle. Savvy professionals take full advantage of this opportunity, because they know it may be the only chance they have to talk with certain people. Once seated, they are primarily responsible for talking with the persons to their right and left. It is inconsiderate to ignore one's immediate dining partners in favor of those one deems more interesting or important across the table.

At the table, diners wait until all—or at least most—table companions are ready to sit down before they sit down themselves. They allow the host to indicate where they should sit, or if there are place cards, they sit accordingly. Diners enter their chairs from the chair's right side to avoid colliding with persons seated to their left. In the business arena, where the focus is not on gender distinctions, men do not pull out women's chairs or rise when they rise. However, if a woman (or a man) receives such treatment, she (or he) accepts it gracefully.

Once everyone is seated, guests wait for the host to remove his napkin from the table before doing so themselves. If the host neglects to do so once everyone is seated, diners may discreetly place their napkins in their laps. At fine restaurants, guests take in stride that servers may drape their napkins across their laps for them. The request for a dark-colored napkin may seem reasonable to avoid lint on one's clothes or lipstick or food stains on one's napkin, but it is not advised. The restaurant may not be able to accommodate the request, and it could come across as a bit persnickety.

Posture at the table is important. Sit up straight, but not stiffly, with both feet on the floor. When engaging in conversation, turn your head, not your whole body, to the person with whom you are speaking. Keep elbows and forearms off the table, and control nervous habits such as drumming fingers, tapping utensils against glasses, and excessively stirring drinks. When drinks or food arrive, wait until the host lifts his glass or a utensil before lifting yours. The host may offer a welcoming toast, and often glasses are clinked, but this is not necessary at business meals.

Napkin Etiquette

A napkin, of course, goes in the lap. If it is a large folded napkin, the crease goes toward the waist. A smaller napkin may lay flat in the lap. Never flap your napkin in midair to unfold it. During the course of a meal, if you wish to take a sip of a drink after having taken a bite of food, dab the corners of your mouth with your napkin first. This avoids the possibility of errant crumbs landing in or on the rim of the glass. Never tuck your napkin into your collar or belt or hoist your tie over your shoulder or tuck it into your shirt to protect it.

If you must leave the table for a moment, your napkin is placed on the seat of your chair, which indicates you are returning. Some people do not like the thought of placing a napkin where they and others have sat, and this is understandable. However, a soiled napkin placed back on the table can be unsightly for other guests. The server may also infer from this placement that you have left and proceed to clear your place setting. At an upscale restaurant, a napkin left on the chair will be quickly refolded by the server and replaced to the left of the plate or draped over the arm of the chair.

The most important thing to remember about napkins is to please use them! Licking your fingers or using the tablecloth to wipe them off is simply uncivilized behavior. Once the meal is finished, the host will place his napkin loosely folded to the left of the plate. Guests then do the same.

Silverware

There are many different styles of eating around the world, but the styles encountered most often in the U.S. are the American and Continental. In the American style, the fork is held in the nondominant hand, which for most is the left hand, and the knife is held in the dominant hand. The diner cuts his food, places the knife on the right side of the plate, blade facing in, and switches the fork to the other hand to eat. Food is scooped with the tines of the fork up. Only one kind of food, such as meat, vegetable, or potato, is eaten at a time. The American style calls for the hands to be placed in the lap when not holding silverware

In the Continental style of eating, the utensils are held in the same fashion as in the American style, but after cutting, the food is speared or pushed onto the fork with the knife and is immediately brought to the mouth, tines of the fork down. More than one kind of food can be on the fork, although the bite itself should not be too big. When resting between bites of food, the Continental style allows for the wrists to rest on the edge of the table.

The question about which style is preferred in the U.S.—American or Continental—comes up often. The answer is the style with which one is most comfortable. Many people like the Continental style because it seems elegant and efficient. Others like the American style because the angle of the fork allows for greater ease in eating some foods, especially those that lend themselves to being scooped such as peas, rice, and corn. Either style is perfectly acceptable, as is alternating between the styles, depending on the food.

The order of the use of silverware is simple: Start with the utensil farthest from the plate. If the table has been set incorrectly, use the utensil you know is correct. If you are missing a utensil, it is appropriate to ask for it. You can tell from the way the table has been set how many courses will be offered and in what order they will arrive. For a three-course meal of soup, entrée, and dessert, you will find a soupspoon to the far right of your setting, a knife next to the soupspoon (to the soupspoon's left but to the right of the plate), and a fork to the left of the plate. Above the plate will be a dessert spoon with its handle to the right and directly below it, a dessert fork with its handle to the left. If you are ordering your own courses, the correct utensils will be brought to you for each course.

One of the most mentioned dining pet peeves is the way in which people hold their utensils. It is difficult to ignore someone holding a fork in a clenched fist or encircling its handle as if it were a flute. Spoons are often held in similarly inappropriate manners, and some diners use their knives like saws. It may be challenging to overcome lifelong bad habits, but with practice it can be done.

A spoon is held properly by placing the thumb on top of the handle at its widest part and placing the handle of the spoon between the first and second fingers. This allows one to spoon soup away and sip from the side of the spoon.

A fork starts out in the nondominant hand, tines down, with the forefinger on the back of the handle and the tip of the finger no farther down the handle than to where the handle and tines meet. If the fork is switched to the dominant hand, as in the American style, the tines are up, and the utensil is held as one would hold a pencil.

A knife starts out in the dominant hand for cutting. Similar to the way in which the fork is held, the forefinger comes down the back of the handle to no farther down than where the handle and the blade meet. In the Continental style of eating, the knife is used to help secure food onto the fork. In the American style, the knife is placed down on the plate, blade facing in, and the fork is switched to the dominant hand to eat.

Once silverware is picked up from the table, no portion of it rests on the table again. If a diner wishes to rest between bites of food, the silverware is placed in a resting position. I favor a resting position of the inverted "V" with the tines of the fork facing right, tines down, and the blade of the knife facing left, blade in, as if to form a tent. Some employ the resting style of the fork on the lower portion of the plate facing left, at about the 5 o'clock–8 o'clock position, and the knife on the upper portion, facing the same way at about the 2 o'clock–11 o'clock position. Either position is fine as long as the server and other diners have a clue as to what someone is trying to signal with his silverware.

When you are finished eating, make this clear by placing the fork and knife next to each other, knife above the fork, with blade facing in, in a 10 o'clock-4 o'clock position. The tines of the fork may be up or down. Most important, do not strew the silverware haphazardly about the plate.

The Crystal

The most important thing to remember about crystal is that if it has a stem, it is held by the stem. If it doesn't have a stem, it is held by the glass, or bowl, in the middle to bottom area, not near the rim. A large-stemmed red wine glass may certainly be held near the base of the bowl to make sure it is steady, but a white wine glass is held in the middle of the stem to avoid warming the wine with the heat of the hand. Do not hold the wine glass by its base or cupped in the hand as you would a brandy snifter.

Dining Decorum

Rich can't *wait* to share his success. And the annual meeting of the retail sales managers of the national chain Yardley Auto Parts is just the place to do it! Rich's store is beating sales records by huge amounts. He decides this is the perfect chance to tell the new company president all about it. He will stand out from the sea of 150 managers while the president is still getting to know the staff.

Rich makes his rounds, chatting with other attendees, all the while searching the tables to see where he is seated. Sure enough, his place card puts him at a table at the opposite end of the room from the president's table. Confident the meeting planner placed the cards randomly, Rich decides he will surreptitiously switch his place card with one at the president's table. Rich can't help but smile, pleased with this brilliant plan.

The meal is about to begin, and Rich sits down at the head table with the president. Just as he starts his conversation with his fellow diners, he feels a tap on his shoulder. It is the meeting planner. "I'm sorry," he says. "You are seated at table 10. You have to move." His cheeks burning red hot with embarrassment, Rich stumbles to stand up and quickly walks to his seat at the far end of the room.

Rich stood out, all right, in a way neither he nor the new president would ever forget.

Seating and Conversation

The guest of honor, if there is one, is seated to the host's immediate right. The second-ranking guest is to the host's left. If there is a cohost, he sits at the opposite end of the table from the host, with third- and fourth-ranking guests to his right and left, respectively. All other diners are seated in the middle of the table. The host speaks with the guest of honor first and at some point during the meal, "turns the table" to speak with the second-ranking guest. All other diners follow suit as well as they can, speaking with the available persons on either side of them.

While conversations between two people work best, there will occasionally be an uneven number of diners or odd seating configuration at the table. Sometimes several people will be involved in one discussion. If everyone remembers their primary conversation responsibilities, no one will be ignored or excluded.

Appropriate conversation topics over business meals are the same as they are for all business encounters. This means avoiding any that are potentially divisive or personal. If you are upbeat, show genuine interest, listen well, and interject humor whenever possible, you will be a sought-after dining companion. Laughter, interest, and enthusiasm are all welcome at business meals. Boredom, negativity, and fatigue are not. You must "sing for your supper" or stay home.

Toasting

If done well, toasting is an extraordinarily powerful tool. Unfortunately, business professionals miss countless opportunities to honor clients and colleagues with words of praise or thanks. Toasting is actually easier than you might think. It simply involves sharing a sentiment that is well thought-out, sincerely and briefly. That's it. Some people avoid making toasts because of the enormous pressure they feel it puts on them to be at once brilliant, original, and hysterically funny. Even professional comedians and speakers can't always hit that high a mark. Just remember to keep the spotlight squarely on the honoree when making the toast and you will relieve yourself of a great deal of pressure.

TOASTING GUIDELINES

- **The host makes the toast.** It occurs after the main course has been cleared, during the dessert course. The host stands and says, "May I have your attention please? We are here tonight in honor of . . ." At a small gathering, the host may stay seated. For a short toast, the host may hold his glass throughout; for a longer one, he may pick it up at the end.

- **The host invites attendees to raise their glasses.** In the U.S., it is appropriate to toast with wine, champagne, or water. All raise their glasses in the direction of the guest of honor and do not clink their glasses among themselves. The honoree is the only person who does not raise a glass; it is incorrect to drink to oneself.
- **The honoree reciprocates.** A toast of thanks is offered to the host and to everyone who has attended by the honoree. All join in, raising their glasses to the host.

Challenges

Challenging situations come up at every meal, and savvy diners handle them deftly. You should call as little attention to them as possible and ignore them if you can. Never embarrass a dining companion by belaboring an incident.

THE PROPER RESPONSE

- **If you drop something on the floor,** leave it there—whether food, silverware, or a napkin. If the item is a hazard, such as a fork in a main traffic area, place it under the table. Do not use it or place it on the table again.
- **If you find something inedible in your food,** such as an olive pit, bone, or gristle, or worse, a bug or strand of hair, quietly bring it to the server's attention. Do not upset dining companions by sharing this information.
- **If you have food stuck in your teeth,** take a sip of water or quietly excuse yourself and tend to it in the restroom. If

you see something on another's lip, chin, or tooth, address discreetly. Point to your mouth with raised eyebrows or whisper the information.

- **If you must cough or sneeze,** turn away and down toward your elbow or over your shoulder. You needn't leave the table, unless you have a prolonged attack or need to blow your nose. Never use a napkin as a handkerchief, but if unavoidable, ask for a replacement.

- **If you spill a beverage,** right the glass, blot the spill, and ask for a clean napkin. Pick up spilled food with a clean spoon or knife, or fingers if necessary, and put it on the plate. Leave crumbs on the table; the server will attend to them.

- **If your guest drinks too much alcohol,** be discreet. Quietly arrange with the server to not offer or pour any more alcohol. If you are not sure your guest can safely drive, insist on driving him home or call a cab.

Dining Dos and Don'ts

There are a number of telling behaviors in business dining situations that distinguish those who have taken the time to learn the intricacies from those who have not. Here are some important tips.

THE DOS

- **Remember, your bread plate is to the left of your plate, and your drinks are to the right.** The acronym BMW, for bread, meal, and water, is a great way to remember this.

- **Cut no more than one or two bites of food at a time.** Take small bites and swallow any food in your mouth before taking a sip of a drink. Chew with your mouth closed. Once food is on your utensil, put it immediately into your mouth.

- **Check coats and umbrellas when possible.** Purses, briefcases, papers, eyeglasses, mobile phones, and medication should be kept off of tables.
- **Avoid food choices that may be problematic to eat.** Save lobster, ribs, and tacos for dining with friends and family. Familiarize yourself with the ways in which to eat various foods.
- **Pay with a credit card** or a standing account. Do not pay with cash.

THE DON'TS

- **Treat restaurant servers or staff disrespectfully.** Executives often take prospective employees out to meals not to see how they treat them, but to see how they treat the servers.
- **Use your fingers to push food.** Don't slurp, burp, or smack your lips.
- **Announce your food likes, dislikes, allergies, or latest diet.** Never complain about the venue, the food, or the service, especially if you are a guest. Do not comment on food choice, offer dietary advice, or monitor consumption. Do not ask to taste others' food.
- **Move or rearrange a place setting** for your ease in eating. Do not wipe off spotty silverware or crystal, rotate your plate, or push your plate away at the end of the meal.
- **Ask for a doggie bag,** whether host or guest, even if the server mentions it.

Throughout the meal, diners carefully and silently monitor the tempo and tenor of the meal to make good judgments about what to do next. If they notice that everyone has finished a course, they put their utensils in the finished position as well. If everyone else orders a drink, first course, and dessert, they do, too. Of course, they do not have to order exactly what others order, but participating in all courses and drinks keeps the pace of the meal even and allows others to enjoy what they wish without fear of rushing or holding others up.

REMEMBER

- Understand the connection between business dining and relationships, reputations, and financial rewards.
- Execute host and guest responsibilities faithfully.
- Practice the mechanics of the business meal.
- Observe all elements of dining decorum.

chapter 9

the social side of business

Knowing the Basics for Every Situation

"A man's manners are a mirror in which he shows his portrait."

—JOHANN WOLFGANG VON GOETHE

Jared had it made in the shade. A top student in a prestigious MBA program, he had just landed a coveted summer internship at a prominent financial services company. Jared knew all he had to do was ace this internship and a six-figure job offer was guaranteed him upon graduation.

All the interns were invited to a welcome-to-the-firm dinner in the luxurious, usually off-limits, executive dining room. Jared ordered a glass of fine Merlot, even though the hosts had preordered wine for the dinner. He enjoyed the wine thoroughly, ordering two more glasses before the main course arrived. When Jared's meal came, it was not cooked to his specifications— he'd ordered his steak medium-rare, *not* medium, he curtly reminded the server—so he sent it back. While he waited, he asked for another glass of wine.

Now confidently holding court at his end of the table, Jared proudly shared his achievements with whoever was within earshot. With a barely detectable slur in his words, he spared no detail about the numerous awards he'd received and the work he'd put into achieving his stellar GPA. Throughout the dinner, Jared jumped into conversations when they interested him, always relating the topic to his accomplishments, and checked texts when he was not interested. Toward the end of the meal, Jared noticed many eyes were on him. Terrific, he thought. They're impressed! That they were appalled was completely lost on him. If the executives had any doubts about offering him a future full-time position, this dinner put that question to rest. Jared had miserably and, unknowingly, failed this crucial test.

The social side of business encompasses everything from a cup of coffee to a five-course meal, and savvy business professionals are comfortable in all of these social situations. Regardless of the formality of the event, the same guidelines for hosts and guests apply, as do all of the dos and don'ts of dining: Arrive early, do not use electronic devices, and correctly handle the silverware, crystal, and napkin. The only thing that changes is the venue.

Entertaining Clients

Advertising executive Emily often entertained clients at breakfasts, taking them to her elegant city club with its beautifully appointed dining room with fresh flowers, immaculate white table cloths, attentive service, and magnificent panoramic views of the city below from the 36th floor. Her guests were always impressed. But today, she was in her new prospect's city. It had taken her months to get on her calendar, and her prospect had made it clear that her schedule was very tight. When she suggested breakfast, Emily quickly and happily agreed. She's always had great luck at business breakfasts! But where?

It had to be distinctive, convenient, and suitable for a business conversation. Emily knew she had one chance to impress this prospect and had to get it right. She did some online reconnaissance and found a charming bistro close to her client's office. The website showed off its lovely décor and people in business suits engaged in conversations. It looked ideal!

Emily arrived early but was immediately told there was a 15-minute wait—and her prospect was already on her way. When they were finally seated, it took another 10 minutes to get coffee and menus. The server was rushed, telling them that they were shorthanded. Thirty minutes after they sat down, their orders arrived, eggs cold and toast overdone and rock hard. Their water glasses and coffee cups remained empty as Emily tried in vain to get the server's attention.

Her prospect announced she really had to get back. She gathered her things, thanked her host, and left. Emily could not even walk her to the door, never mind back to her office, as she waited for the bill. Emily left glum, realizing she had accomplished nothing but wasting her prospect's valuable time. Lesson learned: A pretty website does not ensure a great experience. Emily had failed to do enough due diligence and lost out on promising business in the process.

Coffee

Meeting a client or prospect for coffee is a modest investment of time and money and a great way to make introductions, further relationships, or discuss ideas in an informal setting. Once, coffee was almost exclusively associated with the morning, but now virtually any time of day that works for your client is appropriate for coffee.

You can make this mode of entertainment special from the very beginning by picking your guest up at her office. You eliminate potential issues of transportation or traffic, which could affect arrival times, parking, and seating, and the bonus is that your guest will feel valued. If you use your own car instead of a hired car, make sure it is spotlessly clean and odor-free. An additional nice touch is to have bottled water and possibly mints or hard candy available. A friend of mine in real estate does this and tells me that these small gestures are noticed and appreciated every time.

If picking your guest up is not feasible, ask her in advance what you can order for her. This saves time when schedules are tight. Arrive early to scope out a table. In a self-serve environment, invite your guest to sit, then place and pay for your orders. Offer your guest both something to eat and drink, and follow suit so she feels comfortable in partaking.

Choose a venue that is conducive to a business conversation. Meeting at a private club or café where the staff knows you, where good service is guaranteed, and where you can handle the bill out of sight is ideal. Engage in small talk until the coffee arrives, then introduce the business topic you want to discuss. Keep your voice low in places where you might be overheard.

Coffee is, of course, meant to be quick and casual. Ask your guest how much time she has, keep an eye on the clock, and let her know when the time for her departure approaches. If the conversation is going well, she may extend it. If not, your guest will appreciate that you have been respectful of her schedule. As always, thank your guest for joining you.

Breakfast

More formal than coffee, breakfast is a great way to secure valuable in-person time with clients and prospects in a cost-effective, time-sensitive way. Clients are often more relaxed at breakfast, the challenges of the day not yet having consumed their attention. And if your client happens to work on billable hours or has a hard stop at the end of the day, breakfast may be the only time you can see him. Breakfast is quieter and more personal than later meals, and the service is usually swift.

Breakfast meetings can begin as early as 6:30 A.M. and go as late as 8:30 A.M. If your guest orders something to eat, follow suit, but order foods that are manageable, quick, and healthful. It will not go unnoticed if your guest has a nonfat yogurt with fruit and you have a breakfast of bacon, eggs, and home fries, with a tall stack of pancakes on the side!

Engage in small talk until the coffee comes, then switch to business. When the food arrives, either reintroduce casual conversation or keep the business topic going. Time is of the essence at breakfast meetings, and it is not incorrect to talk business throughout.

Lunch

Lunch meetings are meant for relationship-building and business talk in equal measure. Lunch, more formal and more social than coffee or breakfast, is also more expensive and takes more time. It is a greater investment on the part of your client as well, a testament that you are worth the time!

Midday meals differ in other ways as well. Over lunch, a host offers his guest a cocktail or wine, although in the U.S. this offer will generally be declined. The days of the three-martini lunch are long gone, and it is rare, but not unheard of, to drink alcohol at lunch. Still, in some parts of the country, and at some venues, the offer of beer or wine at lunch may be welcomed. In cultures where drinking at lunch is customary, guests may also take you up on this invitation. Generally, it is best to make the offer, recognizing that you do not need to join in unless you want to. Never drink alcohol at lunch if your guest is not drinking.

Another way lunch differs from coffee or breakfast is the point at which the topic of business is broached. The host begins by engaging in small talk, transitioning to business talk after the meals are ordered and prior to their arrival. Once the meal arrives, he reverts to lighter topics of conversation. Business talks may be picked up again after the main course over coffee.

When business talk is the main purpose of getting together, lunch in the boardroom, the executive dining room, or even the company cafeteria can make good sense. Savvy hosts know that even these venues present golden opportunities for them to make great impressions on their guests. If food is delivered to a meeting room, having real glasses, plates, silverware, and napkins available makes hosts stand out. Guests notice and appreciate not having to grapple with plastic forks, flimsy paper plates, cracking plastic cups, and barely useable napkins. If lunch is in a cafeteria, a host walks through the food lines with her guest or meets him at the cashier to pay for their food. A very nice touch is to arrange to have a company higher-up stop by the table to greet a special guest. A host would make the introduction and facilitate a brief conversation. It is one more chance to let a guest know how valued he is by the organization at all levels.

Tea

One of the best-kept secrets among business entertaining cognoscenti is afternoon tea. The ambiance of an elegant dining room overlooking a beautiful vista, with white linens on the table and a gleaming silver tea service at the ready, is hard to beat. Warm scones, crustless tea sandwiches, assorted sweets, and a reviving cup of freshly brewed tea form a welcome scenario for many a harried businessperson. Tea has all of the elements of a lavish entertainment experience, including sophisticated surroundings, superior service, and excellent food, but little of the expense.

Entertaining over tea reaps great personal branding rewards for hosts who are seen as creative, cultured, and respectful of others' time. Afternoon tea is offered at venerable hotels and restaurants in almost all big cities, and most do a splendid job.

Drinks

Hosts can make the most of the relatively brief time they have with clients over after-hours drinks by giving a great deal of thought to the venue. A good choice is a high-end restaurant where you are known to the staff. There, you will be greeted and welcomed by name at the door and can introduce your guest to the restaurant captain. Your party can then be seated at a reserved table where complimentary cocktail accompaniments such as nuts and olives are often served and drink orders swiftly taken.

If your guest orders alcohol, you as host would follow suit but would limit your consumption to one drink. Sometimes a host may offer his guest another cocktail, but only after acknowledging the guest's presumed time constraints. If the guest is in no hurry and the host's schedule allows, he may suggest dinner, for both hospitality and safety reasons. Too much alcohol on an empty stomach is a recipe for disaster, a scenario with which the host does not want to be associated.

The superb service, ambience, and drinks in this setting make your guest feel honored and set the stage for a wonderful, enduring relationship.

Dinner

Dinner is the most social of business experiences. It is also the one that involves the greatest investment of time and money. In the U.S., dinner with a client usually comes after a business relationship is well underway. But there is still a great deal to learn about business partners over dinners—their histories, their personal lives, and their goals. There may be even more to learn than a host bargained for if alcohol is involved and inhibitions are lowered. Bonds are either cemented over business dinners—or permanently fractured. It makes sense to treat this opportunity with the kid gloves it deserves.

In addition to all of his other host responsibilities, at dinners, the host has one more: the ordering of wine. This is a responsibility he undertakes not only because it's his job, but also because there are risks associated with relinquishing the wine list. Countless sales reps have had to pay exorbitant bills after having trustingly invited their guests to choose the wine. A host also orders the wine because he does not want to put undue pressure on his guest, who may be embarrassed to admit he knows little about wine.

A host should always be aware that when alcohol is involved, people often do and say things they regret or, worse, drive under the influence. A host must be keenly attuned to his guest's condition and do all he can to allow him to save face without contributing to his intoxication. This could mean quietly working with the server to stop offering alcohol or engaging in a lengthy dessert course with lots of coffee.

Dinners are an especially important part of entertaining international guests, who consider them the perfect opportunities to evaluate potential business partners. However, among locally based associates, clients, or prospects, it's important to remember that business dinners can cut into precious family and personal time. If you are meeting a client on her home turf and it is anything but a working dinner, it is considerate to invite her spouse as well.

Wine

At a famous French restaurant in Boston, my host, a wine collector, ordered a $300 bottle of wine per the sommelier's suggestion. The sommelier decanted the wine and, when it was time, poured a small amount in my host's glass for him to taste. When the sommelier asked how the wine was, my host told him he thought the wine had turned. The sommelier then tasted it and announced that my host was mistaken, that the wine was perfectly good. What ensued was a polite yet tense exchange between two individuals both highly knowledgeable on the subject of wine.

Ultimately, the sommelier took the wine back, and my host ordered another bottle at the same price point, which turned out to be fine. The experience for me was a somewhat unnerving joust between two experts. It was the first time I had witnessed the high stakes of the world of fine wine.

One of the most pleasurable aspects of business dinners and life in general is wine. Widely enjoyed, wine is still intimidating to many. Lengthy wines lists, confusing terminology, vastly divergent prices, and the not-so-vague feeling that everyone knows more about the subject can send an otherwise confident business professional straight to the beer list.

While the knowledge of wine can be passionately pursued, you needn't become a Master of Wine to do just fine with any wine list you encounter. This is very good news, because this designation is very hard to come by. According to the Institute of Masters of Wine, there are currently only 342 people in the world who have achieved Master of Wine status.[1] Of those who meet the arduous qualifications to sit for the grueling exam, only 10 percent pass. Master of Wine Jancis Robinson, who achieved the designation in 1984, said, "Master of Wine exams were for masochists when I took them . . . what is stunning is how popular this form of torture is today."[2]

Take heart, no one knows all there is to know about wine. Unencumbered by this pressure, you can instead educate yourself about wine and then blissfully enjoy it to your heart's content. You can read books, take courses, and learn about wine categories. You can attend wine tastings, download apps, and subscribe to wine publications. You can also ask to speak with a professional, as I did with Ashley Waugh, sommelier and general manager of the award-winning No. 9 Park restaurant in Boston, who kindly gave her imprimatur on the advice that follows. These steps will enable you to know as much about wine, if not more, than the vast majority. And they will ensure you are never cowed by a restaurant's wine list again.

A WINE PRIMER

- **Table wine.** Known as still wines, they contain only the juice of grapes. Table wines are bottled after fermentation, the process that converts the sugar of juices to alcohol. In the U.S., table wines, which are drunk with foods, are 7 percent to 14 percent alcohol. In Europe, table wine is defined as the most generic type of wine, sourcing grapes from all around the country. This type of wine cannot carry with it a varietal or region of origin on its label. Alcohol by volume (ABV) can range from 5 percent to 17 percent.
- **Fortified wine.** This wine is strengthened with brandy or a spirit during its fermentation and is popularly consumed as an accompaniment to dessert. Fortified wines are 16 percent to 23 percent alcohol.
- **Aperitifs.** These are flavored wines such as vermouth or Dubonnet. Aperitifs are often served before meals. Herbs, barks, roots, and other flavorings give aperitifs their distinctive flavors. Aperitifs are 15 percent to 20 percent alcohol.
- **Sparkling wine.** Champagne, Asti Spumante, and sparkling Burgundy are in this category. Sparkling wines get their

bubbles through the refermentation of still wines or the addition of artificial carbonation. Sparkling wines are 5.5 percent to 17 percent alcohol.

Most wines are described as white, red, or rosé, with the exception of fortified wines. White and red wines get their color not from the color of the grapes but from the ways in which they are made. White wines are made by simply pressing the grapes to extract the juice. Red wines are made by allowing the juices to ferment in contact with grape skins. Rosés are made by allowing juices to ferment with grape skins for a short time. Champagne, which is always a blend of wine, is categorized as brut (very dry), extra dry (less dry than brut), demi sec (slightly sweet), and sec or doux (very sweet). Popular white wines include Chardonnay, Riesling, Sauvignon Blanc, Pinot Gris, and Pinot Grigio. Popular red wines are Cabernet Sauvignon, Merlot, Pinot Noir, Syrah (or Shiraz), and Zinfandel.

The Regions

Excellent wines are found throughout the world. The most well-known regions include:

- **France.** French wines are named for the regions from which they come. Bordeaux comes from Bordeaux, Burgundy from Burgundy, and Champagne from Champagne. Other regions include the Rhône River Valley for red wines and the Loire Valley and Alsace region for white wines.
- **Germany.** German wines come from the valleys of the Rhine and Moselle rivers. Rhine wines, which come in

brown bottles, are full bodied. Moselle wines, which come in green bottles, are light and off-dry.

- **Italy.** Italian wines may come from Tuscany, Piedmont, or Sicily. Italian red wines include Chianti, Valpolicella, and Bardolino. Italian white wines include Soave and Orvieto.
- **United States.** American wines are named either for the grape (varietal) or the European wine they resemble. Most American wine is made in California, although today wine is produced in all 50 states.

Other well-known wine producing regions include Austria, Australia, Chile, Greece, Spain, Hungary, Switzerland, and Portugal.

Aging

White wines are usually ready to drink as soon as they are bottled. Exceptions include great wines from Bordeaux and Burgundy. Red wines require time to age properly, with the exception of Beaujolais Nouveau. Wines from Spain, Portugal, and Italy may be ready to be consumed within a year or two, but fine French wines may need 10 years. Champagne is best when consumed between 10 and 15 years of bottling.

Ordering Wine

When ordering wine at a restaurant, always ask for the server or sommelier's suggestions, regardless of your level of knowledge about wine. They will (or should) know which wines pair best with their menu selections. This way, you will get an excellent suggestion within your price range. To do this, point directly to a wine on the list, and ask the server what she thinks of that particular wine with the meals that have been chosen. She now knows your price range. Even if she has a different suggestion, she will offer you one close in price to the one you pointed out.

Making sure the wine you are about to serve your guests is good requires you to take some steps. When the unopened bottle is presented to you at your table, first look at the label to ensure it is the wine and vintage you ordered. Once opened, look at the cork. Be sure it is neither soaked through nor crumbling, as either could indicate an issue with the wine. Once a small amount is poured for you to taste, swirl the wine with the base of the glass on the table, sniff the wine, and then taste it. If all is well, the server will pour first for your guests and then for you.

How necessary are all these steps? The chance that the wine you ordered is bad is perhaps greater than you think. It is estimated that for wines with corks, anywhere from 2 percent to 10 percent have been "corked" or tainted. This means they have been contaminated by a chemical compound known as TCA, created by fungi that infected the cork and seeped into the wine. You will know if a wine is corked by its musty or moldy smell. Wine can also be oxidized, or exposed to air, which gives it a vinegary smell. It can be "cooked," or exposed to heat, which makes it taste like stewed prunes. It can be refermented, or could have undergone a second fermentation in the bottle, which leaves it fizzy or bubbly. The proliferation of wines in bottles with screw tops and plastic stoppers have eliminated the chances they are corked, but these bottles can still be affected by improper handling and storage. Screw tops and plastic stoppers do not imply inferior wine. Good wine is also found in boxes, although, as far as I know, boxes of wine have not yet found their way to the business dining table.

Do taste the wine, but put affectations aside. At a business dinner, don't "chew" the wine or make audible noises or contorted facial expressions. If you suspect something is wrong with the bottle, politely ask the server, not your guest, to taste it. At a reputable establishment, the server will take the bottle back without further ado even if he disagrees with your assessment. However, you are not allowed to return a perfectly good bottle you chose on your own simply because you didn't like the taste, especially if that bottle is half empty! But if the server suggested it, and you truly do not like it, it is perfectly acceptable to let him know. A restaurant's primary concern is its customers' happiness. Besides, if it's good, the wine will not go to waste.

White wine does not need to breathe and is best served chilled. Young red wines, those under eight years old, are strong in tannic acid and need to breathe or be exposed to air for an hour or more. Mature red wines need no more than 30 minutes to breathe, and very old reds may not need to breathe at all. However, some sommeliers believe in advance decanting of some Burgundies and Barolos to allow them to "wake up" after long aging. Red wine is served at cellar temperature. White wines are served before red wines; dry wines are served before sweet wines. Champagne may be served at any time before, during, or after the meal.

Wine pours vary from three to six ounces, and the size of the glass will have a bearing on how high it is filled. A red wine glass, which is usually larger than a white wine glass, is filled no more than halfway. This allows the wine "nose," or fragrance, to be captured in the empty space. A white glass may be filled one-third to two-thirds full, depending upon its size.

Traditionally, white wines were served with fish, chicken, pork, and veal, and red wines were served with meat, heavier dishes, and cheese. These rules have been relaxed to accommodate personal preferences. But as you educate yourself about wine, learning about tried and true food and wine pairings will be helpful.

Of course, not everyone drinks wine. If you happen to be one of those individuals and are hosting a business meal, still offer your guest wine, but suggest she order it by the glass, or employ the server to make a recommendation. You need never explain nor apologize for not drinking alcohol, whether for health, religious, or personal reasons. Instead, order what you'd like. If you would prefer not to have to fend off questions, have sparkling water with lime. No one will know it's not a gin and tonic.

If you do drink wine, familiarize yourself with wine terminology: vintage, varietal, acid, tannins, balance, body, nose, legs, etc. Know what dry, fruity, chewy, oaky, earthy, buttery, and velvety mean. Learn how to pronounce wine names. All of this information will allow you to ask intelligent questions about the wine and to understand the descriptions the server offers. There are a number of online resources to help you, including a website by Master of Wine Jancis Robinson, jancis-robinson.com.

Not a wine drinker? Not to worry. Drinking beer is fine at many restaurants, especially casual venues that serve burgers, ribs, or pizza. If this is your choice, drink your beer from a glass that is filled in one pour, not from a bottle or can that is left on the table. But at fine restaurants when everyone else is drinking wine or alcohol, you may decide to sip sparkling water instead of standing out from the group by drinking a beer.

Tipping

Familiarity with tipping guidelines is one more indication of a host's sophistication and generosity. The standard for restaurant servers is now 20 percent of the pretax bill, adjusted higher or lower for the quality of service. But remember, many service issues, such as backed-up kitchens and incorrectly prepared food, are out of the server's control. When seated at a bar, tip 15 percent when only drinks are served and 20 percent if food is included. If it is a buffet where a server brings you drinks but you serve yourself food, 10 percent to 15 percent is appropriate. Coat-check personnel are tipped $1 to $2 per coat; restroom attendants, $1 to $2; doormen, $2 to $5; and car valets, $3 to $5 upon car delivery. For a tip jar at a casual restaurant, contribute at your discretion. Do remember to have a supply of small bills on hand. Having only a $10 or $20 bill is not a sufficient reason to withhold a tip, and it's extremely awkward to ask for change.

Activities and Events

Larry is reluctant to accept a golf invitation from a prospective vendor. He loves golf and would be thrilled to get out on this course, but there is something about the guy that rubs him wrong. Maybe it's the not-so-subtle digs he takes at his competitors, or the "special" pricing he offers Larry that *no* other client gets, or the borderline inappropriate way he talks to Larry's administrative assistant. Still, Larry likes the service this vendor's company offers. He realizes he may be rushing to judgment and decides four hours on the golf course will give him an insight into the man's character one way or the other. And so he accepts.

Two hours into the game, Larry has all the information he needs. He knows as well as anyone how frustrating golf can be but has never seen such poor sportsmanship. When this would-be vendor is not whining, cursing, or throwing his clubs, he is giving other golfers advice and even talking on his cell phone. And although Larry can't prove it, he is pretty sure the guy is cheating. Larry is glad he accepted the invitation because it has made his decision crystal clear—he will never do business with a company who employs this kind of person.

Sporting Events

A sporting event is a wonderful way to further a relationship with a client, whether you and your guest are participants or spectators. These events are entertaining and relaxing and offer the opportunity to develop common interests and bonds. Additionally, sporting events usually last at least two hours and sometimes the better part of a day, afternoon, or evening, providing rare uninterrupted time with valued clients or prospects.

HANDLING THE BASICS

- **If you are a participant,** strictly adhere to the guidelines for attire and play for the event. Your good sportsmanship will be under the microscope.
- **If your guest is a participant,** let him know ahead of time what equipment he will need, what to wear, who else might be accompanying you, and how long the event will take.

- **If you and your guest are arriving separately,** deliver your guest's ticket to his office the day of the event or meet at a designated time and place and hand the prepaid ticket to your guest. Do not pay for any fees or tickets in your guest's presence.
- **If talking business, take your guest's lead.** She may just want to enjoy the event and save business discussions for another time.

The Private Box

Entertaining guests in a private box lets them know that they are held in high esteem. It is critical that the hosts take great care with their duties and that guests also do their part. Hosts arrive early to greet guests, appropriately attired in either high-end business casual or suits if they are coming directly from the office. They offer guests refreshments, introduce them to others in the box, and facilitate small talk.

Boxes are divided into two spaces: one, an enclosed area for mingling and partaking of refreshments, and the other, actual seats for viewing the game. In this intimate gathering, hosts and guests talk with everyone, much as they would at a party. It is acceptable to let others know who you are and what you do, but do not engage in heavy business discussions or obvious sales tactics. Once in the seats, talk business only if your guest initiates it. In this close setting, boisterous behavior or overindulging in alcohol will be noticed and will not be forgotten.

Cultural Events

If you know your guest particularly enjoys cultural events, selecting a concert, a play, a symphony, or an opera will boost you into the business entertainer hall of fame. Scoring hard-to-find tickets demonstrates your thoughtfulness and generosity, and also your ingenuity and influence. Arrange for dinner beforehand, and attend to your guest's comfort throughout the event to create an experience—and relationship—for the ages.

Colleagues

A manager due to speak at an employee awards dinner had had, unbeknownst to her boss, too much to drink. When she was called to the stage to recount the accomplishments of one of the award recipients, she stumbled up the stairs, seeming to barely make it to the podium. There, she immediately launched into a roast of the honoree with rambling, inappropriate remarks, laughing uncontrollably at her own jokes. When no one laughed with her, she told the assemblage to "lighten up." The manager then abruptly shifted her tone and began to engage in an overly emotional tribute to the award winner, choking up tearfully as she described his character and accomplishments. After thoroughly embarrassing herself and her audience, she was escorted off the stage. All eyes were on her as she walked out of the event, her grim-faced boss beside her. She was not fired on the spot, but her position was eliminated a relatively short time afterward.

You've outdone yourself in the business entertainment arena. Now it's time to kick back and enjoy yourself with your colleagues. After a long week, quarter, or year, you look forward to meeting up at a local watering hole or attending a company-sponsored party or event. You've earned this chance to let your hair down with team members and possibly even take advantage of face time with company higher-ups. What could possibly go wrong?

Whenever we are with our colleagues, our brands are on display. And whenever alcohol is served, our good judgment and professionalism are on display, too. Socializing with colleagues in a setting that sounds, tastes, looks, and feels like a party lulls employees into thinking it *is* a party. In fact, it is the most treacherous professional terrain they will ever encounter. The boss who hits on his subordinate, the employee who complains about his salary, the employee who spreads gossip to sabotage a coworker, the employee who belligerently argues his political views, the two teammates who conspicuous flirt then mysteriously disappear—none of this goes unnoticed.

At formal company events, employees who accept an invitation and don't attend, or don't formally accept and *do* attend (sometimes with uninvited guests), are as problematic as those who come too early, too late, or dressed inappropriately— or who spend the entire evening on their electronic devices.

BEST BEHAVIOR

- **Respond promptly to an invitation.** Go if you have accepted. A great deal of time, effort, and expense is involved in any event. To cancel at the last minute or to skip the party entirely (except in the case of an emergency) is extremely inconsiderate.

- **Do not ask to bring a guest.** If you are invited to bring a guest, and do, his behavior and dress reflects on you. A preparty briefing about who's who and what you hope to accomplish is time well spent.
- **Greet hosts and senior persons.** Do not involve them in lengthy conversations, however, as they need to circulate among all of the guests. Take the opportunity to talk with those you may not see on a daily basis.
- **Be enthusiastic!** Participate in the event's activities, and encourage others to do so as well. But remember, it is not your job to be the "life of the party." Email or send a note of thanks to the host the next day. It will be appreciated and perhaps the only one he receives.

Many times impromptu social events will pop up such as drinks with colleagues, casual dinners, and activities such as shopping, walks, and bike rides. The advice is to consider going to as many of these as you can without impacting your work-life balance. They represent terrific ways to bond with coworkers, glean useful information, and generally keep up with what's happening within the organization. Expenses associated with such occasions are not normally covered by the company, so be prepared to pay an equal share, even if you are not drinking alcohol.

Never become the company freeloader. At after-hours drinks with their team, one colleague was always the first to grab the check and divvy up the amount due per person. All contributed their fair shares, no questions asked, until one day someone noticed that the "banker" was the only one who did not contribute to the bill. He also kept the change for himself! Needless to say, this was the last time he was in charge of the bill. No word on whether he was invited for drinks again.

We've learned how much skill is associated with business dining and entertaining. We may have been swayed to consider that there could be life outside of cyberspace and that interacting face-to-face might actually be enjoyable. In fact, we may just be encouraged enough to put our electronic devices down, at least for a moment, and bask in the warmth of real-life smiles.

REMEMBER

- **Entertaining clients and prospects is an art.** Hone this skill and undertake it with deliberation, and it becomes an incredibly powerful professional tool.
- **Wine is an important element of business entertaining.** Learn about wine, and appreciate the relationship-building opportunities that come with this knowledge.
- **Entertaining special people in special ways creates enduring bonds.** Distinguish yourself as a business professional by entertaining in sophisticated settings.
- **Socializing with colleagues is work, not play.** Build rapport within the bounds of unassailable conduct, as this is the course for professional success.

chapter 10

new frontiers

Future-Proofing Your Career

"Real generosity towards the future lies in giving all to the present."

—ALBERT CAMUS

At 64, Louisa is about to go on her first job interview in 40 years. After a rewarding career as a high school French teacher, it's time to retire, but she's not ready to sit on the porch watching the world go by. She loved teaching, but now she asks, "What else can I do?"

Completing an online skills inventory, Louisa was surprised to find out how many skills she had acquired over the years. Communication and listening skills had been a big part of her job as a teacher, of course, but she had never given any thought to how much time she had spent leading, mediating, planning, analyzing, and problem solving. Her excellent people skills meant she was able to relate to everyone, and she was even current with her tech skills—a big bonus. Her best friend, Mimi, the high school's Spanish teacher, came upon the perfect match for Louisa's skills and interests.

Mimi and Louisa roamed the world together during their many summer vacations, and this got Mimi thinking. "What," she asked Louisa, "were the things we always did no matter where we traveled?"

"You mean shopping?" Louisa said with a laugh. "Well, after shopping and sightseeing," she continued, "we went to every gallery, saw every ballet and concert, and went to all of the museums."

"That's it!" Mimi said, "Why not look at a new career in the art world, in a museum? I even know someone right here in our city you could call."

That's how Louisa landed her interview as an arts education coordinator for the city's museum of fine arts. First, she packaged her résumé to align her skills with the responsibilities of the job. She became thoroughly versed in art terminology and familiarized herself with the museum's current and future exhibitions. She also got up to speed on what was happening in other major museums around the world.

Quietly confident but excited, Louisa dresses impeccably and arrives early and ready on the day of her interview. She immediately hits it off with her interviewer, and they share stories of their world travels and the museums they had both visited. Louisa's interviewer suddenly reveals a pleasant surprise. "I want you on my team. When can you start?"

The Future Workplace

Tomorrow is coming. In some cases it is already here. Technological advancements, increased automation, outsourcing, and a concept of work largely defined and designed by and for millennials will shape the near future of our professional lives. This will happen in ways we cannot yet truly comprehend. The good news is that the interpersonal skills you have mastered so far will position you well for what comes next. But you will need to exhibit even greater judgment and dexterity in deciding when, how, and to what extent to employ them.

Wedded as we are to technology, it will never replace the need for human connection. In the future workplace, technological skill will be common among all employees and no longer a distinguishing competitive advantage. What will distinguish individuals is what has distinguished them throughout time: the ability to establish respectful relationships.

In its 2016 Evolution of Work study, ADP Research Institute says there are five overarching trends employers need to know about: choice and flexibility, real-time learning, increased autonomy, stability, and personally meaningful projects. The report also finds that the workplace will see increases in global recruiting, contract hiring, social media collaboration, mobile device-centered work, flexible retirement, flat corporate structures, work-life integration, and technology-monitored productivity.[1]

In his *Forbes* article, "Ten Workplace Trends You'll See in 2016," Dan Schawbel writes about an increase in the rehiring of baby boomer retirees, either as consultants or to take on leadership roles. He sees a revamp of parental leave as 80 million millennials embark upon a baby boom of their own, and he also sees a redesign of office spaces to accommodate workers' preferences.[2]

Jacob Morgan, author of the *Forbes* article, "The Future of Work Is About Flexibility, Autonomy, and Customization," has created the acronym FAC: *flexibility* to work where, when, and how one chooses, *autonomy* to be responsible for one's work effort, and *choice* to work on projects that are most individually meaningful.[3]

In her article in *Fast Company*, "What Work Will Look Like in 2025," Gwen Moran says the jobs that will be most in demand are those that require emotional intelligence such as sales positions, those that are hard to automate such as health care and personal services, and those requiring trade skills, or specific training, such as science, technology, and math.[4]

Among the challenges for professionals in the future workplace is an acceptance of the fact that job security no longer exists—there is no gold watch for 25 years of faithful work. In her *Daily Mail* article, "Will YOUR Job Exist in 2025?" Jenny Awford quotes Martin Chen, chief operating officer of Genesis Property, a real estate developer in China. Chen says that "experts now believe that almost 50 percent of occupations existing today will be completely redundant by 2025."[5] As artificial intelligence, robots, drones, and smart machines continue to redefine the workplace, jobs requiring repetitive tasks are particularly at risk. Higher skilled jobs in the administrative, clerical, and production areas are also on the chopping block, along with the roles of tax preparer, loan officer, and insurance appraiser.

Stress levels will be high and burnout will be a widespread problem as companies and employees try to do more with less time, money, and resources.

Yes, *burnout*, a term introduced in the 1970s, is rearing its ugly head again. In her *Forbes* article, "Overcoming Burnout: Five Ways to Get Back on Track at Work," Vicky Valet quotes Christina Maslach, Ph.D., professor of psychology at the University of California, Berkeley, and author of the "Maslach Burnout Inventory." Dr. Maslach says, "It's not just that people have a bad attitude, it's that they are working in a socially toxic workplace." She says it is not primarily workload, time pressures, and exhaustion that cause burnout; it is a lack of workplace civility. "Something as little as someone rolling their eyes can wear away at you. It's also sarcastic tone of voice, being nasty and rude. It's what you say, how you say it, and how you act."[6]

Two separate 2015/2016 studies by Willis Towers Watson, a global risk management and insurance brokerage, offer another view. These studies indicate that employers and employees alike think insufficient staffing is a major contributing factor to burnout, but they disagree on its other top causes. Employers rank lack of work-life balance and technology that keeps employees tethered to their work as the biggest stressors, but employees say low pay and organization culture are the real issues.[7]

Burnout has dramatic personal and organizational consequences, impacting physical and mental health, employee absenteeism, tardiness, and productivity.

Communicating and collaborating across divergent schedules and time zones with team members and business partners, some continents away, will require enormous flexibility and well-honed communication skills. Members of the "gig economy" will find the number of bosses with whom they will need to get along expanding exponentially. The allure of being one's own boss will be quickly balanced by the realization that each new client brings a new boss, and sometimes decisions are made by a team with multiple stakeholders.

Gloria Larson, president of Bentley University, says, "Specialty skills, which were once assigned to dedicated positions, are now expected and required across several job categories." Social media skills will be required of everyone, not just those on the marketing team.[8] Richard Newton, author of the book *The End of Nice: How to Be Human in a World Run by Robots,* says, "The profoundly human skills of interpersonal communication, empathy, and compassion, along with others such as creativity, problem-solving, and caring, are the ones people will get hired for in the future."[9]

By having a respectful attitude, professionals can develop the soft skills of communication, empathy, and collaboration that their future success requires. Professionals will also need agility to quickly change gears when necessary; humility to admit what they do not know; generosity to help others in need; tenacity to see projects through; courage to deal with uncertainty; tolerance to work with people of different ages, cultures, and levels of experience; good judgment to keep things in perspective; kindness to encourage others; and resilience to try, fail, and try again. A sense of humor and sufficient rest, nutrition, and exercise will also help.

THE FUTURE-PROOF CAREER

- **Take responsibility for your future career.** Know that you are now responsible for creating and managing your career, where once employers dictated career paths and next-step promotions.

- **Commit to continued career development.** Take advantage of free company training or invest in training at your expense and time. Stay current on industry trends and changes, follow thought leaders, and nurture your professional network. You could repackage your skills as a consultant, trainer, or freelancer.
- **Hone your interpersonal and technical skills.** Understand that these are the nonnegotiable assets for success now and in the future.
- **Consider a new career.** Know what you like and what you are good at—then prepare to do it. The future holds great opportunity for creative boutique businesses.

The workspace has undergone dramatic changes. Designed to increase productivity, inspire creativity, facilitate collaboration, and promote health and well-being, workspaces are beginning to look more like homes, gardens, and pubs than the soulless, monochromatic grids of the past. If you happen to work for Deloitte, the professional services organization, in its new Montreal office space unveiled in late 2015, you have 18 different workspaces from which to choose. In addition to a personal workstation (with or without a treadmill), you have quiet rooms, flex spaces, lounges, cafés, bistros, outdoor spaces, fitness facilities, and a concierge at your disposal.

Companies understand workspaces have a great impact on employee experience and help them attract and keep key talent. They also know that the more comfortably and efficiently they allow for work-life integration, the happier, less stressed, and more productive their employees will be.

Employees need to respect their employers' intent in providing on-site amenities. One client said that literally nothing is safe from being taken home at her company, from food, drinks, and supplies to toilet paper! Such unprofessional work behaviors do not go unnoticed by employers and coworkers.

Many now no longer choose to fight traffic to get to the office. Using electronic devices and team collaboration tools such as Slack, they do their jobs wherever they are. Those who want or need space for meetings, a sense of community, or a roof over their heads on a temporary or occasional basis, can use shared office space as an option. Organizations such as WeWork provide monthly rental of desks and private offices. Business is booming. Founded in 2010, this organization now boasts 109 locations in 30 cities around the world. Freelancers, entrepreneurs, and knowledge workers are huge fans of this shared office concept. Businesses also see the benefit, especially for their remote workers.

However your workplace is configured, your brand is always on display. This means being aware of your surroundings and of those you might inadvertently disturb with audible conversations, noise-emitting electronic devices, or wafting food aromas. It also means paying attention to your attire, grooming, and everyday behaviors. By attending to such seemingly small considerations as holding doors open, keeping common areas clean, and being professionally cordial, you will be viewed as an all-star office mate. There could also be ancillary benefits, as that person next to you might be the source of your next great idea or a potential client!

Gen Zs

It has been a particularly exhausting week, and Dan, manager of recruiting, is weary. A lengthy email had just come to him from the vice president of Human Resources, ending with "I'll need your report and recommendations next week. We need to understand these Gen Zs and what we have to put in place to attract them."

In his 37-year career in commercial insurance sales, Dan has worked with three generations in addition to his fellow baby boomers. He has listened to countless stories about the early days from the firm's 76-year-old founder, has commiserated with the boomers about whether they will ever be able to afford to retire, has reassured his 40-something colleagues that they are not being overlooked in favor of tech-savvy millennials, and has tried to keep up with the millennials' constant need for positive feedback.

Dan is simply worn out by the disparate, never-ending expectations of an employee base that spans more than 50 years. And now his boss tells him he has to start planning a strategy for ways to attract an entirely new generation—Gen Z.

Dan knows this is going to be a huge challenge, compounded by the firm's 20th century corporate culture: Old school values, hierarchical management, and pay-your-dues-and-you'll-get-promoted thinking prevail as surely as they did when the company was founded. Sure, they have installed the obligatory foosball tables and now offer unlimited snacks to keep millennials quiet, but these are merely stopgap measures. The company has an enormous amount of catching up to do, especially if it wants to compete for the most talented members of this new generation. Maybe the expectations of Gen Zs will provide the push the company needs to finally get into the 21st century.

Dan writes his report, addressing the challenges the firm will face in appealing to this huge new cohort as well as the expensive initiatives they will need to offer. He just hopes they don't shoot the messenger.

No discussion of the future of work would be complete without an eyes-wide-open look at the next generation knocking at the door. Most agree Gen Z is the first generation of true digital natives. The oldest of them are just a year or two away from joining the workforce. Born approximately between 1994 and 2014, Gen Z could be some 60 million strong and is poised to redefine the workplace once again.

Who are the Gen Zs? According to Anne Kingston's article "Get Ready for Generation Z" in *Maclean's*, "They are smarter than Boomers, and way more ambitious than Millennials," and are "educated, industrious, collaborative, and eager to build a better planet."[10]

"Meet Generation Z: Forget Everything You Learned About Millennials," a presentation by the New York advertising agency Sparks & Honey, says members of Gen Z are mature, future thinking, humble, realistic, and entrepreneurial. They embody a collective social consciousness and value education and working for success. They like live-stream media such as Twitch and Ustream and communicate via FaceTime and Skype. Gen Zs also have challenges that may be related to the extent of their electronic device use: short attention spans, a lack of situational awareness, imprecise communication, and obesity.[11]

Gen Zs, known also as centennials, iGeneration, and Homeland Generation, are thought to be far more private and pragmatic than their millennial brethren. The children of Gen

Xers, they have seen the problems brought on by over-sharing on social media and prefer sites like SnapChat and Whisper to the permanency of Facebook posts. Having lived through global conflict and the Great Recession, Gen Zs are also considered cautious, serious, and prone to worry.

Constant Connectivity

Hannah's mom is worried about her 20-year-old daughter. She wonders what ever happened to the energetic, happy young girl she once was, the girl who would come bounding through the front door after school eager to share her day's activities or her newest crush, with her cheeks ablaze after soccer practice. Hannah's mom remembers a healthy, athletic young woman brimming with vitality, cheer, and confidence.

Over the past year, everything has changed. Her daughter now has bags under her eyes, has gained weight, and is so pale. Hannah's college grades are falling. And she never seems to leave the house! The few times her mother actually sees her, Hannah seems depressed.

Hannah's mom gets up her courage *again* and knocks on her daughter's door. She knows her concerns will not be well received, but she believes her daughter's life is at stake and she just can't ignore it. "I'm *fine*, mom. Just leave me alone!" yells Hannah from behind the closed door.

But something is clearly wrong, and Hannah's mom is convinced it has to do with the amount of time she spends on her devices. She's heard stories about the online bullying, the shaming, the trolling, and she knows that in some cases, these activities have had tragic consequences. If she could just talk to her daughter, face-to-face, she could find out what's going on and maybe help.

So she knocks. And knocks. And knocks. After five minutes, the door opens. Hannah emerges from her room, seemingly resigned to a conversation and maybe just a tiny bit relieved. "Okay, let's talk," she says.

Constant connectivity brings real risks to users' work, privacy, relationships, and health. Most of us know this intuitively, but few of us actually believe that these risks apply to us. In the article "Health Benefits of Unplugging and Going Screen-Free This July 4," *The Huffington Post* reports "over-engagement with social media can cause anxiety [and] feelings of low self-esteem."[12] A ceaseless barrage of photos of people engaged in awesome activities with their awesome friends can elicit feelings of jealousy, insecurity, and loneliness in those not similarly engaged. Increased social media activity often comes at the expense of decreased physical activity with weight gain and sleep affected as a result. A study from the website Science Daily found that the blue light of a tablet lowers melatonin, the sleep hormone.[13]

Online activity also harms relationships, interpersonal communication skills, and mental health, according to Sophie Breene, author of "Why Everyone Should Unplug More Often." She says research indicates that "social media is the millennials' 'drug of choice' and to many in this cohort, a self-described addiction."[14] Other potential problems include depression and poor posture, as well as sight, circulation, digestive, and skin issues. It can also cause wrist, neck, and other muscle strain.

The Unplugged Life

Did you know there is a National Day of Unplugging? Starting on the first Friday each March, participants pledge to unplug from technology for 24 hours. An outgrowth of the Sabbath Manifesto, the National Day of Unplugging is meant to encourage one day a week to "unwind, unplug, relax, reflect, get outdoors, and connect with loved ones."[15] Its website, nationaldayofunplugging. com, offers resources and news about events, as well as some of the many great reasons people choose to unplug.

In 2010, the World UNPLUGGED project polled students from around the world who gave up social media for 24 hours. They reported feelings of freedom, liberation, peace, and solitude, and they had more time to engage in creative thinking, be with family and friends, talk, listen, read, enjoy the sunshine, laugh, eat, drink, chat, wander, jog, walk through the park, listen to the birds, and engage in hobbies.[16]

Digital Detox

John can't believe it. His company is coming up to the end of a very challenging quarter with sales goals unmet and now wants the management team to go on a "digital detox" retreat—whatever that is. "Why now?" John thinks. He is irritated. Every quarter, it takes a Herculean effort on his part to push his team to the finish line. Constant email status updates, texts of encouragement and warnings in equal measure, and links to the fabulous resort they will be going to if they come in first are just some of the ways he keeps them motivated.

Sure, he may rely a bit heavily on technology to keep his staff on task. And yeah, it's been a while since he's "seen" his teenaged kids other than on social media or "spoken" with his wife during the day other than by text. But that is just the way things are these days. This is not the time for him to be without his devices, especially for an entire weekend!

But knowing he needs to get on board if he wants to stay employed, John makes the trip to the beautiful campsite a few hours away. Dutifully complying with the rules, he turns his devices and watch over for safekeeping until the end of the retreat. At first, John literally does not know what to do with his hands. He reflexively checks his pockets for the phone not there and looks at his naked wrist where his watch used to be. "This is going to be hard," he thinks.

In the common area, John takes a look at the activity board. A nature walk, hmm, that might be a good way to take the edge off. Archery? He hasn't done that since summer camp. Then there's yoga—that's something he's always wanted to try. John spies a colleague and is ready to commiserate about their forced getaway, when his relaxed-looking colleague tells him excitedly that he's getting ready for the hike. Does John want to come? After the day's activities, there is an evening around the campfire with an outdoor buffet, a corny but fun sing-along, and talks about their plans for tomorrow.

Maybe this isn't so bad, John thinks. He has forgotten about reaching for his phone and the quarterly sales figures. Looking forward to the next day's activities, he'd love to try his hand at printmaking and is not going to miss the scavenger hunt and tug-of-war. And he has a surprise for his colleagues at tomorrow night's talent show: It's high time they knew what a great singer he is! After an exhausting day in the fresh air, John is ready for sleep. He drifts off thinking about all the fun that awaits him. But he also knows, when tomorrow comes, if he chooses, he can do nothing at all but breathe in and out and look at the gorgeous scenery surrounding him. Nice!

THE DIGITAL DETOX

- **Declare your independence.** You are not your technology. It is a tool. You have control.
- **Start slow.** Designate a time each day to power down. Fill that time with other activities: yoga in the morning, meditation in the afternoon, dinner with family or friends in the evening, reading a novel before bed. Work up to a tech-free half or full day.
- **Reduce temptations.** Engage in activities that make the technology virtually impossible like skiing, cycling, swimming, cooking, painting, sculpting, dancing, knitting, board games, tennis, or playing the tuba. Work on a crossword or jigsaw puzzle.
- **Cut down on social media checks.** Limit yourself to once or twice a day. Discover how little you miss it. Use an away message to let others know you are fine, just momentarily unreachable. Emergency messages will get through.
- **Ban technology from the bedroom and dinner table.** Make it off-limits in conversations.
- **Take advantage of apps.** Apps such as Offtime and Checky are designed to help you observe and limit your tech use.

Mark Zuckerberg of Facebook said, "Every year, I take on a personal challenge to learn new things and grow outside my work at Facebook." In 2016, he announced he would run 365 miles at the pace of one mile a day. In 2015, he vowed to read one book every two weeks. "I've found reading books very intellectually fulfilling. Books allow you to fully explore a topic and immerse yourself in a deeper way than most media today."[17]

The Eternal Truths

"Boy, is he going to get an earful from me!" yells Matt, the owner/manager of a busy city copy shop, to his long-time employee, Leslie, and to anyone else within earshot. On any given day, he would have requests for a dozen rush jobs in addition to his regular customers' orders. Matt is actually glad for the rush jobs because when people are in a hurry, they don't mind paying more to go to the head of the line. "It's great for business—and business is great," he always says.

But there is one problem: the local delivery company he uses for these jobs. Matt has given them an enormous amount of business over the years, mostly because they are the only game in town. But WeDeliver's employee turnover rate is high—really high—especially among its bicycle couriers. This means inexperienced workers and lost, late, missed, and damaged deliveries. On countless occasions, Matt has had to refund the money of many an angry customer and provide complimentary services just to keep them coming back.

Matt has complained dozens of times, and the owner of WeDeliver always promises to do better. But within a week, it is back to the same problems, accompanied by calls from unhappy customers. Matt has threatened to take his business elsewhere, but that's an empty threat—there *is* no other place to take his business. In fact, Matt is pretty convinced the delivery company owner doesn't even take his complaints seriously anymore.

So for the second time this week, the fifth time this month, and who knows how many times this year, Matt calls the owner with his usual frustrations and dissatisfactions. Afterwards, Leslie, his quiet, loyal, long-time employee, asks Matt if she can offer a suggestion. Gently reminding him of how many years this has been a problem, and the toll it has taken on them all, she asks, "Why don't we hire our own delivery person?"

Merriam-Webster defines *eternal truths* as "valid for all time." The phrase is usually associated with the words of major historical and cultural figures whose teachings have stood the test of time, such as Socrates, Aristotle, and René Descartes. Aristotle said, "We are what we repeatedly do. Greatness, then, is not an act but a habit." The principles in George Washington's *Rules of Civility: The 110 Precepts That Guided Our First President in War and Peace* also provides examples of such timeless counsel. Inspired by the writings of Jesuit tutors, our first president copied out these rules and carried them with him as a guide for his life and work.

The precepts include the following:

> "Wear not your clothes foul, ript or dusty, but see they are brush'd once every day at least, and take heed that you approach not to any uncleanliness."[18]

Translation: Attire and grooming matter greatly!

Do eternal truths exist in today's professional arena? By observing behaviors over a long period of time that result in similar outcomes, perhaps we can lay claim to our own set of personal truths. The year 2017 marks 22 years for me in the field of etiquette and protocol. Over these years, I have had the privilege of discussing the importance of respect and civility in the workplace with thousands of undergraduate and graduate students, newly hired employees, and tenured professionals. All have inspired me and shaped my perspective on life and work.

MY ETERNAL TRUTHS

- **Past behavior is a strong indicator of future behavior.** Individuals and organizations can change, but it takes a concerted, consistent effort and a long time to change others' minds about them.
- **Insincerity can be spotted a mile away.** A successful relationship, whether personal or professional, is not possible without both perceived and genuine respect.
- **Everyone deserves the benefit of the doubt.** Adopt the belief that everyone is trying his or her best and you could probably eliminate 95 percent of workplace strife.
- **You will not always be liked.** Do your best and hope for the best in return.
- **Everyone wants to be heard.** You needn't agree, just listen.
- **Things change.** As time marches on, there is no percentage in not also changing.
- **Everyone makes mistakes.** Stress, fear, and fatigue can bring out the worst in anyone. Cut others slack, and while you are at it, cut yourself some slack, too.
- **"I'm sorry" are two of the most powerful and underused words in business.** Acknowledge mistakes and you strengthen relationships.
- **Reputations are fragile.** Take great care with your own and with others' reputations.

- **Time is fleeting.** Think about how you spend your days. You will never get them back.
- **Learning is lifelong.** It's required of us all, and that's a great thing.

What are your truths? Learn to trust your judgment and your gut feelings, and let your experiences and observations be your guide. Act in ways that respect rather than challenge the truths you have observed, both in your life and others' lives, and you will save time, energy, and consternation. This will also allow you to focus on the things you *can* change.

Integrating all of this advice at once may seem daunting, but do not despair. While you are adding to your skills and burnishing your brand, there is a shortcut that can buy you time. One quality above all others will virtually guarantee your personal and professional success, regardless of where you are in your journey. It is the quality of empathy.

Renowned physicist Dr. Stephen Hawking said, "The human failing I would like most to correct is aggression. It may have had survival advantage in caveman days, to get more food, territory or [a] partner with whom to reproduce, but now it threatens to destroy us all."[19] The quality he would most like to magnify? Empathy—because "it brings us together in a peaceful, loving state." Writer George Orwell, also a strong voice for empathy, lived briefly on the streets of London with those on the fringe of society. He wrote about his experience in *Down and Out in Paris and London,* a book still referenced more than 80 years later as one of the most powerful on the subject of empathy.

Practice the skills you have learned consistently. Try to understand rather than judge. Listen attentively and use nonverbal cues carefully. Try to "walk a mile in another's shoes."

Further develop your empathy skills by showing appropriate curiosity, using affirming language, and being fully present in the moment.

REMEMBER

- **Respect is the cornerstone of all successful relationships.** The right attitude is not enough. Respect requires awareness, intention, and execution.
- **Technology is a tool over which we have complete control.** Unplug and look up from your devices. Your health, happiness, productivity, and relationships depend on it.
- **Empathy is the most powerful of all human qualities.** In personal and professional relationships, if you are able to display true empathy, you will succeed.

"Here's looking at you, kid." —Rick to Ilsa in *Casablanca*

conclusion

We have taken a look at the importance of respect and civility in today's workplace from both macro and micro points of view. Depending upon one's age and experience, the information offered here is brand new, familiar, or a combination of both. For all, these pages serve as a reminder that good business manners still matter, even if today they seem scarce or manifest themselves in unfamiliar ways.

But there may be a few lingering questions. For instance, you might agree that all things being equal, interacting respectfully is a good thing. But when critical matters are at stake, can't too much emphasis on "politeness" get in the way? The answer to this question is no. It's when a situation is most precarious that civility is most needed. In fact, a calm, respectful approach may be the only thing that keeps a situation from going from serious to unsalvageable.

You might then ask what the point is of being the only well-mannered person in the room. Couldn't that be considered a sign of weakness? The answer again is no. Maintaining composure, especially when others do not, is a sign of tremendous strength. The person who does this serves as a powerful role model. Even if others are not behaving in a similarly constructive fashion, they are still watching.

Well, at least you can point out when others are being rude, right? As tempting as it might be to do so, the answer is yet again no, for a number of reasons. First, adults are responsible for their own behavior. Good manners preclude an individual from correcting another, with the exception of his underage children, even if his intentions are sincere. Second, there is a slight chance that you are reading the situation wrong. Commenting upon it will underscore this. Third, even if you *are* reading the situation correctly, try to overlook others' transgressions as much as possible. This is a good policy, because it is only a matter of time before you make a mistake, and you'll be grateful that someone does the same for you. Finally, no matter how justified, no one ever appreciates being corrected, especially in front of others. Relationships suffer permanent damage as a result.

But what if someone *asks* for advice or feedback on her behavior? That's okay, isn't it? The advice is to tread very carefully here. If the relationship is a trusted one and the advice is earnestly solicited, you may offer feedback, but only if it is not personally directed. You can say you have employed or observed or read about techniques for handling the situation in question, and let the person distill this information as he sees fit. But do not agree with another's self-assessment of his failings or, worse, point out ones he had not even mentioned.

But don't you run the risk of being seen as inauthentic if you don't offer honest feedback? Only if the content of the message is itself untrue. Careful thought must be given to the wording of difficult messages, but it is nonetheless absolutely possible to get such a point across civilly. In fact, for credibility and professionalism, the calm delivery of a message is always more powerful than an emotion-filled one. Not every attendant feeling has to be shared in the process.

Organizations can certainly put into place rules of conduct, mission statements, and best practices to help guide their employees' behavior. And if individuals are 100 percent sure that they are witnessing disrespect, they can confront it. But even then, it is done by expressing the impact of someone's words or behaviors, not by calling into question his character or calling him rude.

So, even if under extreme provocation, you cannot give in to uncivil behavior or directly correct others who do, you might ask, "What's in it for me?" This is a good question.

To answer it, all we need do is think back upon the times we let our emotions take over. Even though we felt justified at the time, it usually did not take long for remorse to set in. For most of us, our impatience or less-than-courteous words and actions quickly came back to haunt us. What's in it for all of us is not having to deal with such regrets in the future—or at least not having to deal with them as frequently. This is made easier when we remember that someone's bad behavior usually has little to do with us and far more to do with what that person is feeling or enduring at the time.

A friend shared with me this story: While searching for a parking space near his doctor's office, he noticed a parked truck that was taking up two spaces. With no other spots available, he pulled up beside the truck, rolled down his window, and politely asked the driver who was sitting in the front seat if he would mind moving up slightly so he could park. The driver glared at him and angrily told him no, including an obscene gesture for emphasis. Taken aback, my friend nonetheless did not react. After circling for another 15 minutes, he finally found a spot several blocks away and arrived at his appointment 5 minutes late.

When he exited the building 30 minutes later, he noticed the man still sitting in his truck. As he passed by, the man got out of the truck and approached him. Not knowing what to expect, my friend was surprised by what happened next. The man said he had been waiting for him—to *apologize*. He went on to say he was having a particularly bad time at work and that he thought he was about to be fired. However, he said that that was no excuse for his behavior and that he was truly sorry. My friend immediately accepted his apology. He assured him he knew that bad days could get the better of anyone—they had of him in the past. Each left the encounter feeling a bit better—my friend for not compounding the situation by reacting to bad behavior and the man for apologizing for his.

We have outlined the many career benefits that accrue to those who practice the Platinum Rule, including being a part of building a better workplace. But in the end, civility is its own reward. In employing this rule, one's relationships with others vastly improve. But it is the relationship with oneself that benefits most. It is an unqualified win, from every perspective.

acknowledgments

Among the many things I have learned on this journey is that it takes a multitude of talented, kind, and generous individuals to make the idea of a book a reality. I am deeply indebted to my clients and advisors for their encouragement and for the experiences they shared. Some are directly quoted in these pages, others served as inspirations for stories shared and advice offered. My sincere thanks to Amanda Addeo, Wendy-Lee Austin, Barbara Brooks, Anne Calhoun, Andrea Carlson, Lawrence Carlson, Penni Connors, Robert Cuomo, Ph.D., Diane Danielson, Kurt DelBene, Gisele Garceau, Richard Garcia, Tully Hannan, John Heroux, Mike Hines, Kevin Holian, Carmella Kletjian, Sue Kline, Gabriella LaMonica, Katherine McEleney, Patrick Malone, Dan McCarthy, Rosemary Murphy, Alison Quandt, Gary Roderick, Jean Ruggeri, Kristen Scott, Esta Singer, Mark Steinberg, Lynda Stevens, Barbara Thomas, Jon Thomas, Mike Trombetta, Deanna White, and Jackie Wilbur. I also thank Lewis Lapham, Lisa Pierpont, and Michael Salmon for their support and the key introductions they made on my behalf.

I am most grateful to Ellen Kadin, executive editor of AMACOM books, for taking a chance on this fledgling author and to my skilled literary agent, Michael Snell, for his expert guidance and continuous encouragement. My sincere thanks go

ACKNOWLEDGMENTS

to my talented editor, Patricia Snell, for her painstaking efforts and keen direction and to Libby Koponen and Nichole Bernier for their vital editorial contributions.

I am also very grateful to friends who, with unwavering support, have seen me through this process. Special thanks go to Claudia Clark, Ron Clarke, Kathy Gallinaro, Colleen Jerwann, Debbie Monosson, Francis O'Keefe, Ted Patrikas, Vince Spiziri, Janie Walsh, Sara Wilhelm, and Beth Witte.

To all of my Thomas, Hannan, and McCarthy family members for enthusiastically taking this journey with me: a huge thank you. Special thanks to Barbara, Nina, and Robert for their wonderful help and countless pep talks. And profound thanks to Jean, my mother, for too many things to mention. Finally, to Donald, my champion from day one: I could not have done it without you. Thank you.

notes

INTRODUCTION

1 Christine Pearson and Christine Porath. *The Cost of Bad Behavior: How Incivility Is Damaging Your Business and What to Do About It*. New York: Hardcover Portfolio, 2009.

CHAPTER 1

1 Milton J. Bennett (1979). "Overcoming the Golden Rule: Sympathy and Empathy." In D. Nimmo (Ed.), Communication Yearbook 3. International Communication Association.

2 Steve Gruenert and Todd Whitaker. *School Culture Rewired: How to Define, Assess, and Transform It*. Alexandria, VA: ASCD, 2015.

3 Christine Pearson and Christine Porath. *The Cost of Bad Behavior: How Incivility Is Damaging Your Business and What to Do About It*. New York: Hardcover Portfolio, 2009.

4 Mike Miles. "Workplace Bullying Costs Companies Billions, Wrecks Victims' Health." SmartSign blog. December 13, 2012. http://www.smartsign.com/blog/costs-of-workplace-bullying/.

5 Kevin L. Nadal. "Sexual Orientation Microaggressions in Everyday Life: Experiences of Lesbians, Gays, Bisexuals, and Transgender Individuals." PsycEXTRA Dataset. Accessed November 2, 2016. doi:10.1037/e615782009-001.

6 Steve Mintz. "Workplace Values and Expectations of the Millennial Generation." Workplace Ethics Advice, April 28, 2016. http://www.workplaceethicsadvice.com/2016/04/28/.

7   Erik Sherman. "6 Oldest CEOs in America in 2015." *Fortune*, December 12, 2015. http://fortune.com/2015/12/13/oldest-ceos-fortune-500/.

8   Rebecca Riffkin. "Average U.S. Retirement Age Rises to 62." Gallup, 2014. http://www.gallup.com/poll/168707/average-retirement-age-rises.aspx.

9   "U.S. Bureau of Labor Statistics." U.S. Bureau of Labor Statistics, 2015. http://www.bls.gov/.

10   "Center for American Progress." Center for American Progress, 2050. https://cdn.americanprogress.org/.

11   Ibid.

12   "Center for American Progress." Center for American Progress, 2012. https://www.americanprogress.org/.

13   Sarah Kate Ellis. "GLAAD CEO: Tim Cook Is a Game-Changing Exec for LGBT Workforce." *Time*, October 31, 2014. http://time.com/3551490/tim-cook-is-a-game-changing-exec-for-lgbt-workforce/.

14   Steven Petrow. "LGBT Etiquette, by Steven Petrow, the (Mostly) Well-Mannered Syndicated Columnist." Stevenpetrow.com, 2016. http://www.stevenpetrow.com/gay-manners.html.

15   Brandon Bailey. "Facebook Offers More Options for Members to Describe Their Gender." *Mercury News*, February 13, 2014. http://www.mercurynews.com/business/ci_25137519/facebook-offers-more-options-members-describe-their-gender.

16   Miranda Perry. "How to React When Someone Comes Out: Dos and Don'ts for Straight Allies." Care2.com, April 12, 2016. http://www.care2.com/causes/how-to-react-when-someone-comes-out.html.

17   Office of Disability Employment Policy (ODEP). "Disability Etiquette." United Cerebral Palsy, 2015. http://ucp.org/resources/disability-etiquette/.

18   "Disability." Center for American Progress, 2016. https://www.americanprogress.org/issues/disability/view/.

19   John A. Challenger. "Survey: 53% of Employers Concerned About Retirement Plans, Brain Drain." Challenger, Gray & Christmas, Inc., 2016. https://www.challengergray.com/press/press-releases/survey-53-employers-concerned-about-retirement-plans-brain-drain.

CHAPTER 2

1   Peter Dizikes. "Putting Heads Together." *MIT News*, October 1, 2010. http://news.mit.edu/2010/collective-intel-1001.

2   Ken Sundheim. "15 Traits of the Ideal Employee." *Forbes*, April 2, 2013. http://www.forbes.com/sites/kensundheim/2013/04/02/15-traits-of-the-ideal-employee/#2b4a36bd7c94.

3   Vivian Giang. "The All-Time Worst Interview Mistakes Job Candidates Have Made." *Business Insider*, January 16, 2014. http://www.businessinsider.com/worst-job-interview-mistakes-2014-1.

4   "Survey: 60% of Employers Checking Your Social Media." Challenger, Gray, & Christmas, Inc., May 13, 2014. https://www.challengergray.com/press/press-releases/survey-60-employers-checking-your-social-media.

5   Jens Maier. "Corporate Universities." In *The Ambidextrous Organization: Exploring the New While Exploiting the Now.* Springer, 2015. Accessed August 22, 2016. https://books.google.com/books?id=fOcHCgAAQBAJ&lpg=PT137&ots=rJhDYrKaMX&dq=Gil%20Press%20an%20attitude%20by%20businesses%20%2C%20nonprofits&pg=PT137#v=onepage&q=Gil%20Press%20an%20attitude%20by%20businesses%20,%20nonprofits&f=false.

6   Jerome Maisch. "Big Data's Impact on Human Resources." Digimind blog. Accessed August 22, 2016. http://digimind.com/blog/competitive-intelligence/big-datas-impact-in-human-resources/.

7   James A. Martin. "Does Your Klout Score Matter?" *CIO*, January 27, 2014. http://www.cio.com/article/2379266/consumer-technology/does-your-klout-score-matter-.html.

8   Anne Fisher. "The Most Ridiculous Interview Questions." *Fortune* blog, April 5, 2011. http://fortune.com/2011/04/05/the-most-ridiculous-job-interview-questions/.

9   Jacquelyn Smith. "What to Do When You're Offered a Job and You Need More Time to Decide." Yahoo.com, June 3, 2015. http://finance.yahoo.com/news/politely-postpone-accepting-job-offer-175800901.html.

10 John Rossheim. "How to Help Millennials Fill the Soft Skills Gap." Monster Hiring Resource Center. Accessed August 23, 2016. http://hiring.monster.com/hr/hr-best-practices/workforce-management/employee-performance-management/millennial-soft-skills.aspx.

11 Sue Shellenbarger. "Just Look Me in the Eye Already." *Wall Street Journal*, May 28, 2013. http://www.wsj.com/articles/SB10001424127887324809804578511290822228174.

12 Carmine P. Gibaldi. "11 Ways for Older Employees to Stay Relevant at Work." *Business Insider*, August 22, 2012. http://www.businessinsider.com/11-ways-for-older-employees-to-still-feel-relevant-at-work-2012-8.

CHAPTER 3

1   Napoleon Hill. *Think and Grow Rich: Teaching, for the First Time, the Famous Andrew Carnegie Formula for Money-Making.* Meriden, CT: Ralston Society, 1937.

2   Al Ries and Jack Trout. *Positioning: The Battle for Your Mind.* New York: McGraw-Hill, 1981.

3   Tom Peters. "A Brand Called You." *Fast Company*, August 31, 1997. Accessed August 23, 2016. http://www.fastcompany.com/28905/brand-called-you.

4   Dan Schawbel. "Chapter 1: The Brand Called You." In *Me 2.0: Build a Powerful Brand to Achieve Career Success.* New York: Kaplan, 2009.

5   Yesenia Rascon. "Expert Advice: 8 Tips for Building Your Personal Brand—NerdWallet." Nerdwallet.com, June 9, 2014. https://www.nerdwallet.com/blog/loans/student-loans/expert-advice-8-tips-building-personal-brand/.

6   Henry Blodget. "Let's Get One Thing Straight—Apple Had No Choice but to Oust Steve Jobs." *Business Insider*, September 23, 2013. http://www.businessinsider.com/apple-had-no-choice-with-steve-jobs-2013-9.

7   Jim Rohn. "Rohn: The One Thing That Determines How Successful You Can Be." Success.com, May 22, 2015. http://www.success.com/article/rohn-the-one-thing-that-determines-how-successful-you-can-be.

8   Charles R. Swindoll. "The Importance of Attitude." Insight for Living Ministries, July 20, 2015. http://www.insight.org/resources/daily-devotional/individual/the-importance-of-attitude.

9   "A Look at the Shocking Student Loan Debt Statistics for 2016" Student Loan Hero™, Inc. Accessed November 2, 2016. https://studentloanhero.com/student-loan-debt-statistics.

10 Ali Meyer. "Census Bureau: 30.3% Millennials Still Living With Their Parents." CNS News, February 17, 2015. http://www.cnsnews.com/news/article/ali-meyer/census-bureau-303-millennials-still-living-their-parents.

11 Robert Armstrong. "Sorry JPMorgan, Smart Guys Still Wear Suits." *Financial Times*, June 8, 2016. http://www.ft.com/cms/s/0/7b9bb1bc-2d56-11e6-bf8d-26294ad519fc.html.

12 Seth Harden. "Commuter Driving Statistics." Statistic Brain, March 4, 2016. Accessed August 25, 2016. http://www.statisticbrain.com/commute-statistics/.

13 "Distracted Driving: Facts and Statistics." National Highway Transportation Safety Administration/U.S. Dept of Transportation. Accessed August 25, 2016. http://www.distraction.gov/stats-research-laws/facts-and-statistics.html.

CHAPTER 4

1   Tim Kastelle. "Hierarchy Is Overrated." *Harvard Business Review*, November 20, 2013. https://hbr.org/2013/11/hierarchy-is-overrated.

2   Atlassian. "You Waste a Lot of Time at Work Infographic." Atlassian.com. Accessed August 25, 2016. https://www.atlassian.com/time-wasting-at-work-infographic.

3   Anna Codrea-Rado. "Open-Plan Offices Make Employees Less Productive, Less Happy, and More Likely to Get Sick." Quartz, May 21, 2013. http://qz.com/85400/moving-to-open-plan-offices-makes-employees-less-productive-less-happy-and-more-likely-to-get-sick/.

4   Gensler. "2013 U.S. Workplace Survey." Gensler.com. Accessed August 25, 2016. http://www.gensler.com/uploads/documents/2013_US_Workplace_Survey_07_15_2013.pdf.

5   Statistic Brain. "Employee Theft Statistics." Statisticbrain.com, September 7, 2015. http://www.statisticbrain.com/employee-theft-statistics/.

6   Adam Vaccaro. "Your Office's Fridge-Raiders Are Stealing Much More Than Food." Inc.com, April 7, 2014. http://www.inc.com/adam-vaccaro/workplace-lunch-thieves.html.

7   Hajo Adam and Adam D. Galinsky. "Enclothed Cognition." *Journal of Experimental Social Psychology* 48, no. 4 (July 2012): 918-25. doi:10.1016/j.jesp.2012.02.008.

8   Glassdoor Team. "Top 20 Employee Benefits & Perks." Glassdoor.com (blog), February 3, 2016. https://www.glassdoor.com/blog/top-20-employee-benefits-perks.

9   Matt Richtel. "Housecleaning, Then Dinner? Silicon Valley Perks Come Home." *New York Times*, October 19, 2012. http://www.nytimes.com/2012/10/20/us/in-silicon-valley-perks-now-begin-at-home.html.

10 Adam Jones. "The Spies in the Cellar Are Now Sidling Up to

Your Desk." *Financial Times*, December 28, 2014. http://
www.ft.com/cms/s/0/9412d776-89b4-11e4-8daa-00144feabdc0
.html#axzz4IMrGp6Bj.

CHAPTER 5

1   Ben Decker and Kelly Decker. "The Top Ten Best (and Worst)
Communicators of 2015." Decker Communications (blog),
December 16, 2015. https://decker.com/blog/the-top-ten-best-
and-worst-communicators-of-2015/.

2   Brian O'Keefe. "The Man Who's Reinventing Walmart." *Fortune*, June 4, 2015. http://fortune.com/2015/06/04/walmart-ceo-
doug-mcmillon/.

3   Sam Walton. "10 Rules for Building a Business." Walmart.com.
Accessed August 27, 2016. http://corporate.walmart.com/our-
story/history/10-rules-for-building-a-business.

4   Amy Cuddy. "Your Body Language Shapes Who You Are." TED
.com, June 2012. https://www.ted.com/talks/amy_cuddy_your_
body_ language_shapes_who_you_are?language=en.

5   Patryk Welowski and Kasia Welowski. "How Micro Expressions
Predict Success: Patryk & Kasia Wezowski at TEDx UHasselt
Salon." TEDxTalks video, November 13, 2013. http://tedxtalks
.ted.com/video/How-Micro-Expressions-Predict-S.

6   Skills You Need. "Body Language, Posture and Proximity."
Skillsyouneed.com. Accessed August 27, 2016. http://www
.skillsyouneed.com/ips/body-language.html.

7   Lucy Kellaway. "Time to Get Stoked by the Year's Worst Corporate Guff." *Financial Times*, January 3, 2016. http://www
.ft.com/cms/s/0/a989fc5c-aa4b-11e5-9700-2b669a5aeb83.html
#axzz 4IXz6u1OT.

8   Fran Alston. "Decline in Grammatical and Writing Skills of the
New Generation Due to Techspeak." CNN iReport, March 25,
2014. http://ireport.cnn.com/docs/DOC-1112008.

9   Paul Gil. "The Top 30 Internet Terms for Beginners, 2016."
    About.com Tech, June 5, 2016. http://netforbeginners.about
    .com/od/internetlanguage/tp/the-top-internet-terms-for-
    beginners.htm.

10 John Medina. "The Brain Cannot Multitask." Brain Rules blog,
    March 16, 2008. http://brainrules.blogspot.com/2008/03/brain-
    cannot-multitask_16.html.

11 Ryan Weaver. "Multitasking Isn't Possible, So Stop Hurting Your
    Own Productivity by Attempting It." Techvibes, January 31, 2014.

CHAPTER 6

1   Barry Siskind. "Marketing: Technology vs Face-to-Face."
    Salesgravy.com. Accessed August 28, 2016. https://www.
    salesgravy.com/sales-articles/insurance/marketing-technology-
    vs-face-to-face.html.

2   Teddy Wayne. "At the Tone, Leave a What?" *New York Times*,
    June 14, 2014. http://www.nytimes.com/2014/06/15/fashion/
    millennials-shy-away-from-voice-mail.html.

3   Jenna Wortham. "Pass the Word: The Phone Call Is Back." *New
    York Times*, September 20, 2014. http://bits.blogs.nytimes.com/
    2014/09/20/pass-the-word-the-phone-call-is-back/.

4   Verena Von Pfetten. "Read This Story Without Distraction (Can
    You?)." *New York Times*, April 29, 2016. http://www.nytimes
    .com/2016/05/01/fashion/monotasking-drop-everything-an
    d-read-this-story.html.

5   Sarah Radicati and Justin Levenstein. "Email Statistics Report,
    2013-2017." Radicati.com PDF, April 2013. http://www.radicati
    .com/.

6   Alina Tugend. "What to Think About Before You Hit 'Send.'"
    NYTimes.com, April 20, 2012. http://www.nytimes.com/2012/
    04/21/your-money/what-to-think-about-before-you-hit-send
    .html?_r=0.

7 "Distracted Driving." Centers for Disease Control and Prevention, March 7, 2016. http://www.cdc.gov/motorvehiclesafety/Distracted_Driving/index.html.

CHAPTER 7

1 Statista. "Social Networks—Statistics & Facts." Statista.com. Accessed August 30, 2016. https://www.statista.com/topics/1164/social-networks/.

2 Jeffrey Rosen. "The Web Means the End of Forgetting." *New York Times*, July 24, 2010. http://www.nytimes.com/2010/07/25/magazine/25privacy-t2.html.

3 Mark Fahey. "Facebook Costs Trillions in Wasted Productivity." CNBC.com. February 4, 2016. http://www.cnbc.com/2016/02/04/facebook-turns-12--trillions-in-time-wasted.html.

4 Dorie Clark. "How to Repair a Damaged Online Reputation." Huffingtonpost.com, April 21, 2015. http://www.huffingtonpost.com/dorie-clark/how-to-repair-a-damaged-o_b_811000.html.

5 Ryan Holmes. "5 Lessons from U.S. Airways' Social Media Scandal (Column)." Marketingmag.ca, April 22, 2014. http://www.marketingmag.ca/advertising/5-lessons-from-us-airways%E2%80%99-social-media-scandal-column-108394.

6 Scott Stratten. Social Currency in Social Media. Performed by Scott Stratten. YouTube.com, June 3, 2009. https://youtu.be/MjsOwr_whHc.

7 Kevan Lee. "Infographic: How Often Should You Post on Social Media?" Digital image. Sumall.com, February 25, 2015. https://blog.bufferapp.com/how-often-post-social-media.

8 Daniel Bean. "11 Brutal Reminders That You Can and Will Get Fired for What You Post on Facebook." Yahoo.com, May 6, 2014. https://www.yahoo.com/tech/11-brutal-reminders-that-you-can-and-will-get-fired-for-84931050659.html.

9   Marketing Charts. "18-24-Year-Olds on Facebook Report an Average of 649 Friends, Up from 510 Last Year." Marketingcharts .com, March 10, 2014. http://www.marketingcharts.com/onlin e/18-24-year-olds-on-facebook-report-an-average-of-649-frie nds-up-from-510-last-year-41233/.

10   Rachel Dicker. "You Only Have Four Real Friends on Facebook, Study Says." U.S. News & World Report, January 29, 2016. http://www.usnews.com/news/articles/2016-01-29/only-four-facebook-friends-are-your-real-friends.

11   Statista. "LinkedIn: Number of Users." Statista.com. Accessed August 30, 2016. http://www.statista.com/statistics/274050/ quarterly-numbers-of-linkedin-members/.

12   Susie Poppick. "10 Social Media Blunders That Cost a Millennial a Job." Time.com, September 5, 2014. http://time. com/money/3019899/10-facebook-twitter-mistakes-lost-job-millennials-viral/.

13   Chris Brogan. "My Twitter Presence." Chrisbrogan.com, August 12, 2010. http://chrisbrogan.com/my-twitter-presence/.

CHAPTER 8

1   Kevin D. O'Gorman. "Dimensions of Hospitality: Exploring Ancient and Classical Origins." In *Hospitality: A Social Lens*, 17-32. Advances in Tourism Research. Amsterdam: Elsevier, 2007. http://www.academia.edu/279771/ Dimensions_of_Hospitality_Exploring_Ancient_Origins.

2   Christina Ohly Evans. "Jorge Pérez's Dining Boltholes." Howtospendit.ft.com, July 29, 2016. http://howtospendit. ft.com/food/110513-jorge-prezs-dining-boltholes.

3   Simon De Burton. "Richie Nanda's Dining Boltholes." Howtospendit.ft.com, July 10, 2015. http://howtospendit. ft.com/food/87421-richie-nandas-dining-boltholes.

4   Adam Bryant. "Walt Bettinger of Charles Schwab: You've Got to

Open Up to Move Up." *New York Times*, February 4, 2016. http://www.nytimes.com/2016/02/07/business/walt-bettinge r-of-charles-schwab-youve-got-to-open-up-to-move-up .html.

CHAPTER 9

1   Institute of Masters of Wine. "Institute of Masters of Wine Partners with Wine in Moderation." Mastersofwine.org, April 21, 2016. http://www.mastersofwine.org/en/news/index.cfm/ id/E6377FCE-7418-4F83-9C5B24E8A98F3B84.

2   Jancis Robinson. "Masters of Wine." *Financial Times*, September 13, 2013. http://www.ft.com/cms/s/2/c92eb238-1a0 5-11e3-93e8-00144feab7de.html.

CHAPTER 10

1   "The Evolution of Work Study: The Changing Nature of the Global Workplace." Publication. ADP Research Institute, 2016. http://www.adp.com/tools-and-resources/adp-research- institute/research-and-trends/research-item-detail.aspx?id= DF55E8A7-906A-4E81-A941-E886886BC9B2.

2   Dan Schawbel. "Ten Workplace Trends You'll See in 2016." *Forbes*, November 1, 2015. http://www.forbes.com/ sites/danschawbel/ 2015/11/01/10-workplace-trends-for-2016/ #e60b31f222c1.

3   Jacob Morgan. "The Future of Work Is About Flexibility, Autonomy, and Customization." *Forbes*, September 22, 2015. http://www.forbes.com/sites/jacobmorgan/2015/09/22/th e-future-of-work-is-about-flexibility-autonomy-and-customi- zation/#794bd3e32d59.

4   Gwen Moran. "What Work Will Look Like in 2025." *Fast Company*, May 19, 2015. https://www.fastcompany.com/ 3046332/the-new-rules-of-work/what-work-will-look-like- in-2025.

5   Jenny Awford. "Will Your Job Still Exist in 2025? New Report Warns 50 per Cent of Occupations Will Be Redundant in 11 Years Time." *Daily Mail*, November 8, 2014. http://www.dailymail.co.uk/news/article-2826463/CBRE-report-warns-50-cent-occupations-redundant-20-years-time.html.

6   Vicky Valet. "Overcoming Burnout: Five Ways to Get Back on Track at Work." *Forbes*, June 23, 2015. http://www.forbes.com/sites/vickyvalet/2015/06/23/overcoming-burnout-five-ways-to-get-back-on-track-at-work/#5dcf7c1e491b.

7   Willis Towers Watson. "Staying@Work™ Report: Employee Health and Business Success." Willistowerswatson.com, March 10, 2016. https://www.willistowerswatson.com/en/insights/2016/03/stayingatwork-report-employee-health-and-business-success.

8   Gloria Larson. "How to Future-Proof Your Career: Start with Hybrid Job Skills." PreparedU: Careers. Bentley.edu, March 2, 2016. http://www.bentley.edu/prepared/Careers/all?page=7.

9   Richard Newton. *The End of Nice: How to Be Human in a World Run by Robots.* Amazon Digital Services LLC, 2015. https://www.amazon.com/End-Nice-robots-Kindle-Single-ebook/dp/B00W1Y91VC.

10 Anne Kingston. "Get Ready for Generation Z." *Maclean's*, July 15, 2014. http://www.macleans.ca/society/life/get-ready-for-generation-z/.

11 Sparks & Honey. "Meet Generation Z: Forget Everything You Learned About Millennials." Slideshare.net, June 17, 2014. http://www.slideshare.net/sparksandhoney/generation-z-final-june-17/56.

12 The Huffington Post. "Health Benefits of Unplugging and Going Screen-Free This July 4." Huffington Post blog, July 4, 2013. http://www.huffingtonpost.com/2013/07/04/health-benefits-of unplugging_n_3528710.html.

13 Rensselaer Polytechnic Institute (RPI). "Light from Self-Luminous Tablet Computers Can Affect Evening Melatonin, Delaying Sleep." ScienceDaily. August 27, 2012. https://www.sciencedaily.com/releases/2012/08/120827094211.htm.

14 Sophia Breene. "Why Everyone Should Unplug More Often." Greatist, June 24, 2015. http://greatist.com/happiness/unplugging-social-media-email.

15 Reboot. "About." The National Day of Unplugging. Accessed August 31, 2016. http://nationaldayofunplugging.com/about-us/.

16 International Center for Media & the Public Agenda. "About the World Unplugged." The World UNPLUGGED blog. Accessed August 31, 2016. https://theworldunplugged.wordpress.com/about/.

17 Mark Zuckerberg. "Mark Zuckerberg's Facebook Page." Facebook.com, January 3, 2016. https://www.facebook.com/zuck/posts/10102577175875681.

18 George Washington and Richard Brookhiser. *Rules of Civility: The 110 Precepts That Guided Our First President in War and Peace*. New York: Free Press, 1997.

19 Jonathan O'Callaghan. "Aggression Could Be Our Downfall: Survival of the Human Race Depends on Kindness and Co-operation, Says Stephen Hawking." *Daily Mail*, February 19, 2015. http://www.dailymail.co.uk/sciencetech/article-2960508/Survival-human-race-depends-weeding-aggression-says-Stephen-Hawking.html.

index

about the author

ROSANNE J. THOMAS, President, Protocol Advisors, Inc.

Rosanne J. Thomas is a certified Etiquette and Protocol Consultant, and founder of Protocol Advisors, Inc., of Boston, Massachusetts. Ms. Thomas travels the country presenting training programs designed to instill confidence and help professionals achieve their personal goals for success.

Recognized as an expert in her field, Ms. Thomas makes frequent appearances on television, radio, and in print. She was featured in *The Boston Globe's* "Miss Manners on Wall Street," and has contributed to the WCVB TV show *Chronicle,* as well as to WHDH, WBZ, and FOX TV programs. Additionally, she has been interviewed by CBS This Morning, MTV, and National Public Radio and has been featured in articles by *The Wall Street Journal, Newsweek Magazine,* and *Entrepreneur Magazine.* Ms. Thomas' professional background also includes eleven years with the internationally renowned Tiffany & Co.